Save Time,
Save Money,
Save Yourself

Save Time,
Save Money,
Save Yourself

by Dorsey Connors

A Stuart L. Daniels Book

HAWTHORN BOOKS, INC.
PUBLISHERS / New York

To John Edward Forbes,
my skipper

CONTENTS

INTRODUCTION

"The time has come," the Walrus said,
   "To talk of many things:
Of shoes and ships and sealing wax,
   Of cabbages and kings."
                                        —Lewis Carroll

Hi! I'm Dorsey Connors.

For lo these many years, I have been imparting household hints via the telly and a syndicated column. I do believe the time has come to cull the tiptop tips and present them to you, my dear reader, in book form. May they shorten the hours you devote to household chores, stretch your budget, and consequently result in extra time and money that can be spent on sweet, adorable you.

Whether that time and money is expended on a super new outfit, a day at the beauty salon for a "massage-hairdo-the works," or a glorious weekend trip, I'd like to think that I helped you attain it. It's my way of saying "Thank you" for your constant stream of letters, asking me to compile these ideas into a book. Also, many of the hints presented here have been selected from the thousands of letters that cross my desk each week. To these knowledgeable kitchenauts who share their helpful thinking, I am especially grateful.

Treasure this thought: Good housekeeping can put a lot of sparkle in you as well as your home. Think of the physical work as great exercise to get you into fine shape. You'll be surprised to find how this will change your attitude toward the nitty-gritty grind of daily housework. Now, I don't expect you to jump up and down, clap your hands, and shout, "Goody, goody, it's time to scrub the floors." But, truly, if you stretch and bend properly as you work, knowing that you are constantly improving your figure, it might put a smile on your face. And that's an immediate plus for your appearance.

Too, finding faster, easier ways to care for your home, your family, and their clothes, could give you those hours you need for the self-improvement that will recharge your batteries. Be it lessons in Yoga, art, tap dancing, or a back-to-school course in your favorite subject, they all come under the heading of You-Owe-It-to-Yourself.

So, to every matey with a skipper and a crew of tykes, to the bridey-bird about to assume a wifestyle, and to the career chickadee or the bachelor with a single pad to manage, I offer these time-preservers, money-preservers, and life-preservers. Here's to a smoother sailing for your household ship.

Ahoy and enjoy!

Save Time,
Save Money,
Save Yourself

CHAPTER 1

SAVE TIME

Dost thou love life? Then do not squander time;
for that's the stuff Life is made of.
—Benjamin Franklin, *Poor Richard's Almanac*

Ben really summed it up for us, didn't he? To make
good use of every waking moment is not all that difficult if you set your mind to it. Even during those tedious moments when you ride in an elevator, sit in a bus
or a train, or stand in a line at the supermarket check-out
counter, you can be accomplishing something. Use
the time to improve your posture and figure. Pull
your chest well out of the rib cage and tense the
tummy muscles. Relax and repeat! Employ isometric
exercises. The astronauts do these while they're flying
to the moon. You can do the same while you're
chauffeuring the skipper to the station or piloting the
kids to school. Do you turn over in the morning for
a little extra snooze, not because you need the ad-

ditional sleep, but because you have so many things to do that you don't know where to start? That's a no-no, doll. The head-shrinkers tell us we're just trying to escape our responsibilities when we sleep too much. Here's my little plan to relieve those too-much-to-do tensions: First thing in the morning, make a mental list of the things that must be done, another list of the things that should be done, and then a third list of the things you'd like to do. It may sound complicated, but believe me, if you get into the habit of mentally coordinating your activities early in the morning, you'll be surprised how you fly through the have-to-be-dones into the should-be-dones and eventually into the want-to-dos.

Time your household chores. An oven timer will help you do this. For instance, if you like to use a fabric softener but never seem to get to the machine to put the softener in for the second rinse, set your timer and find how long it is from the beginning of the cycle to the second rinse. Then employ the timer as soon as you put the wash in, and when it rings, add the softener.

What would happen if your skipper said, "Honey, where is that electric saw that I won in the golf tournament last year?" Okay, so maybe it isn't a saw. Maybe its an automatic weed puller, or a do-it-yourself car-greasing rack. But he won it, and you never thought he'd use it, so you stored it away in the attic, the basement, or the storeroom. And Tsk, Tsk, Tsk! You don't know where it is, do you?

Well, the next time you reorganize that storage space, establish this system: Mark each box with a number. Attach large sheets of white cardboard to the door or wall of the storage room. On the cardboard place the number of each box and list its contents: Box No. 6—Christmas tree ornaments; Box No. 7—diplomas and ice skates; etc. It'll save many a family feud and your time to boot!

❦

The bathroom mirror is a great place to tape reminder notes.

❦

Use a hanging plastic shoebag with shelves to store yarns. Various colors and textures can be grouped together and are completely visible. Labels from the skeins (for future reference) and instructions for articles to be made can be stored along with the yarns. Also tuck in a few mothballs, just in case Mr. Moth likes the taste of the yarns.

❦

When you drop a contact lens, save a lot of searching time by wrapping cellophane tape—sticky side out—around the palm of your hand and going over the floor area, gently of course. The lens will stick and will not be scratched.

❦

If you secure a nylon stocking over the nozzle of a vacuum-cleaner attachment, you can often retrieve small objects like contact lenses in a jiffy.

❦

Since so many household conveniences have detachable electric cords, storage of the cords has bugged many a person. The simplest and best method is to fold each cord neatly and secure with a twist of a colorful pipe cleaner. The twelve-inch craft pipe cleaners can be used for longer cords.

❦

Appliance cords can also be kept in drawers in an orderly fashion if they are folded to fit within a toilet-tissue cardboard tube. These tubes can be covered with attractive paper, and labeled. Owners of electric knives might be pleased to know that the longer cardboard tubing (from waxed paper, foil, etc.) makes an excellent protector for the blades. Wrap the blades with a dishcloth and slip them into the tubing.

❦

Sew a different colored thread to the top of new stockings before they are worn—a special color for each pair. You'll be able to sort them in a jiffy after washing them.

Slip plastic bread wrappers over your hands before polishing shoes. The plastic is thin enough to allow you to grasp the applicator easily and hold the shoe. Use them also to encase the buffers, brushes, etc., in the shoe polishing kit.

After polishing baby's shoes with white polish, allow them to dry thoroughly and then buff them with a piece of waxed paper. *Voilà!* A nice shine and no more white rub marks on clothes from Junior's little feet.

Make a habit of saving and reading hang tags that come with garments. So many new synthetic materials are on the market that even if you think you have a photographic mind, I've got news for you, baby. You'd have to be a computer to remember all the instructions. Mark the hang tags as you remove them from the garments so you know which is which and then store them in a file box handy to the laundry area.

☙⚬❧

Fill out your personal check while standing in line at the supermarket and you'll only have to insert the amount.

☙⚬❧

Here's a tip that will certainly save wear and tear on new carpeting. Make shoe covers from men's discarded socks. After cutting about three inches off the top of each sock, slit the center about halfway so it slips over a shoe easily. Ties can be made from shoelaces. If workmen come in or the children appear with muddy shoes, they are directed to the utility room where they can put on the sock shoe covers.

☙⚬❧

Keep the measurements of your dining-room tablecloths posted in your linen closet. Measure the table without leaves and then with one, two, and three leaves. When preparing for entertaining, you'll know just which tablecloth is right for the number of leaves used.

☙⚬❧

Use name-and-address labels on both the envelope and the letter inside when you write to request instructions. Always carry a few of these labels in your purse and apply them to the blanks in store contests. (The space provided always seems so small.) Here are other uses: (1) the bottoms of cake plates sent to church bazaars, (2) on books and magazines loaned to friends, (3) on a small piece of cardboard which can be placed under a door if you find no one at home, (4) on plastic raincoats and caps, umbrellas, and luggage (covered with transparent tape for protection).

Keep a nutcracker in a basket with polishes and manicuring implements. When a bottle of nail polish refuses to open, just grasp the top with your trusty nutcracker, and with a twist of the wrist, the bottle is opened.

Here is how to save time and energy in making the bed. Mark the center of the blankets and bedspread with just a few stitches of bright thread at both top and bottom. This saves a lot of readjusting and walking around the bed.

Save yourself many footsteps and a lot of time by following this procedure. When placing freshly laundered sheets and blankets in the linen cabinet, be sure they are folded lengthwise first. Then when you make the bed, place this fold at the center of the bed. The idea is to make the bed completely on one side before moving around to the other.

❦

Annoyed by residue that accumulates in soap dishes? Place a sponge under the bar of soap and use the sponge to quickly wash out the tub or the sink. Always use a few drops of a mild liquid detergent in your bath tub to cut down on bathtub ring.

❦

Unwrap your bar of soap as soon as it comes from the store and place it in bureau drawers. It imparts a sweet, clean odor. The soap dries out a bit, hardens, and strangely enough, lasts a lot longer when used.

❦

Seemingly useless slivers of soap can be tucked into an old nylon stocking and provide a fine bath or shower mitt. Tie the soap-filled foot at the ankle with colorful string. Hang it near the bathtub or shower stall.

❦

Save old face cloths. When you are expecting guests, clean the bathroom and then tuck a face cloth under the soap dish. The wash basin can then be used by the family, and just before the guests arrive, remove the face cloths, give the sink a quick wipe and—presto! —clean soap dishes.

❦

Lipstick on a drinking glass is unsightly and a bother to wash as well. Keep a supply of drinking straws in your kitchen cabinet and whenever you need water for a pill or just for drinking purposes use the straws. Goblets and makeup stay intact.

❦

Invest in a carpenter's apron. When washing windows use the many pockets to carry spray cleanser, cloths, and that indispensable little scraper. No more running up and down the ladder. When doing the daily chores, fill the pockets with polishes and brushes and cloths. On wash day, use the apron to hold lots of clothespins.

❦

Have you too many times ended up in a fitting room with a dress marked with the right size, only to find the garment is too large or too small? Sometimes the discrepancy is due to styling, but often manufacturers have different concepts of sizes. To save time and frustration, carry a tape measure with you. A fast measurement of a garment's vital parts often saves a trip to the fitting room. The same tape measure saves a trip to return merchandise when used to measure slacks, shirts, dresses, etc., for your children.

You may lose your shopping cart in the supermarket as you run to the other side of the store to get a favorite box of cereal. When you trot off to the supermarket, slip a bright ribbon in your purse. Tie it or your scarf to your shopping cart for easy identification.

Keep a styrofoam cooler chest in the trunk of your car. When you buy perishables such as ice cream, butter, milk, etc., have the checkout clerk place these items in one bag and transfer them to the cooler. You can then spend a little more time in town as the products will stay cool and the ice cream will not melt for at least two hours.

In preparing a shopping list put the aisle number of the supermarket in which that particular item is located after each item. So then as you scan the list, you can pick up all the articles listed in each particular aisle. It avoids return trips and saves so much precious time. Or when you make up a shopping list, list the articles to be purchased under their respective categories, such as produce, meat, canned goods, dry foods, soaps and cleansers, personal, etc. It may take a few minutes longer to prepare your list, but it sure saves time at the market.

Carry a snap-type clothespin in your purse. Use it to clip your shopping list to the grocery cart. It not only keeps the list from being misplaced but is also available for consultation by the children if they are helping you shop.

Here's a way to have a glorious fire in the fireplace without worrying about cleaning up the ashes. Cover the bottom of the fireplace with a big sheet of aluminum foil and simply gather it up with all the debris when the fire has burned itself out.

Keep a big calendar in the kitchen right next to the telephone and have a different color pencil for each member of the family. As they make their appointments or as they tell you about them, mark the appropriate colors on the square reserved for that date.

Then each morning you can tell at a glance if anyone in the family has something special to do that day.

Awaken each morning to the sound of a clock radio? In order to eliminate the job of checking each evening to be sure the volume is just right (loud enough to awaken you, but not so blaring as to disturb the neighbors), mark the volume knob with a red marker pen. Check the mark at night.

When you fold your husband's underwear after laundering, place the shorts inside the folded T-shirt. This makes for a neat arrangement in his bureau drawer and a fast selection for him on hectic mornings.

When relining bureau drawers, turn each drawer upside down for measuring and cutting of the liner. It's much easier than trying to fit the inside of the drawer.

Anytime I can find the easy way to do anything, that's for me, and for you, too, I hope. The best way to get out of scrubbing that kitchen sink—and the rubber mats that you may have covering the counters—is to let the stains and dirt soak away. After you finish the dishes, turn that little stopper in your sink. Sprinkle your cleanser in the sink and throw in the rubber mats. Fill the sink with hot water. You sit down and read the paper, while your manicure is being saved, and your sink and mats are soaking clean.

⚜

Those foil containers that hold commercial pie and rolls can act as bibs, surrounding each stove burner, and save a lot of time in cleaning. Cut off the edges and flatten them with a rolling pin. Then cut them to size with a hole in the middle to fit on the top of the range.

⚜

Ever throw out a magazine and then discover that someone wanted a particular article or picture? In order to prevent this from happening (and also to prevent clipping until after everyone has had a chance to read the magazine), staple a piece of blank paper to the front of each magazine when it first comes into the house. Each person jots down the name of the article or page of the picture that he wishes to save. Before you dispose of the magazine you can clip it for the entire family.

CHAPTER 2

SAVE MONEY

O money, money, money. I'm not necessarily
one of those who thinks thee holy,
But I often stop to wonder how thou canst go
out so fast when thou comest in so slowly.
—Ogden Nash,
"Hymn to the Thing That Makes the Wolf Go"

You can save a lot of loot by using some of the
cleansing agents that are probably sitting right on your
shelves, such as vinegar, baking soda, and rubbing
alcohol. Too, you can pinch a few pennies by cutting
down on the amount of detergent that you use for
all washing and cleaning. Learn how little you need
to do an effective job. Most of us use too much. You'll
not only stretch that old budget dollar, but you'll
also feel a warm glow in realizing that you are an
ecological kitchenaut who is helping to save our lakes
and rivers.

Try toothpaste as a substitute for silver polish. It works like a charm. If dinner guests are arriving and there is no time to go to the store, it sure is a help.

✥

Would you believe that a sharp pencil could cut down your locksmith bills? Oftentimes, you may think the lock's tumblers are broken when all the lock needs is a little graphite. The cheap and easy way to do it is to rub a pencil on the edges of your key and insert the key to lubricate the lock.

✥

I once spent an entire morning wrestling with a shower head, but believe me, it was worth it. The skipper has been complaining for nigh onto a year about his erratic shower. The once bounteous Niagara-like flow had dwindled to a tickling trickle.

Rather than spend three weeks indoors waiting for the moment when the plumber might deign to visit (why is it that no serviceman can give you a definite time of arrival?), I decided to tackle the job myself. With a trusty wrench, I detached the head from the shower, unscrewed the front and discovered that the inside was coated with mineral deposits. Using an old toothbrush I scrubbed every cranny of the shower head with hot water and detergent and rinsed it thoroughly. A goodly portion of the deposits still remained.

Now comes my little pearl of shower wisdom, and I pass it on to you for what it's worth. I boiled the shower head in vinegar, using an old pan. Wow! Miracle action! The shower head is as clean as the whistle that I expect to hear when the skipper turns on the faucet tomorrow morning.

❦

If you wash your hair in the shower, place a piece of steel wool over the drain. It will catch any loose hairs that might impede the plumbing. Good to remember, too, for that tub where you wash the dog.

❦

Want some bathroom accessories, but the prices are way above your budget? Look for some finds in your own cabinets—an old sugar jar, a stoppered vitamin bottle, an inexpensive bud vase. Buy some spray enamel for less than a dollar and spray the items in a color that harmonizes with your bathroom decor.

❦

Need some new coasters? Buy two 9-by-9-inch carpet squares and cut each into four equal pieces. You'll have eight colorful, absorbent coasters that do not slide because of the backing. Use the indoor-outdoor carpet squares, as they can be cleaned so easily. If squares are not your bag, you can cut these into circles or other interesting shapes. They also make cute, inexpensive gifts.

❦

Unless you're absolutely balmy about the repairman, don't overload your washing machine. Washer capacities vary, and you should know exactly how much yours takes. If you don't, phone the store where you bought the machine and find out. Most washer breakdowns come from overloading.

❦

Here is a genuine trade secret. Fill your washer with warm water and pour a gallon of distilled vinegar into it. Let the machine run through the entire cycle. The vinegar will cleanse the wash hoses and unclog them from soap scum and save many dollars in repair bills.

❦

Rub petroleum jelly on the heels of your stockings, and boots will slip on with ease. No more rips and runs and the petroleum jelly does not harm the nylons.

❦

Mothers of small children should save the tops of hair-spray cans and similar containers. When you take your brood to the park or beach, these tops become their individual drinking cups. Scrub them thoroughly and enclose them in plastic bags or foil wrap for transporting. Another set can be used as toys for the beach sand.

Can't bear to part with the beautiful bows that come on gift packages? Keep them stored in a box. If they get crushed restore them to their original crispness by preheating your clothes dryer and tumble three or four bows at a time. The result is amazing. The bows look brand new and are ready to again adorn a beautiful gift package.

A small nick in a drinking glass's rim can be smoothed out and made safe with an emery board.

Removing mattress and boxspring covers during housecleaning can be a tiresome chore and costly, too, because the zippers so often break. It's cheaper and easier to use old fitted sheets. Place two on both mattress and box spring—one on the top, the other on the bottom. What used to be a two-man job can then be handled all by yourself.

Wrap seldom-used white linens in blue tissue to prevent yellowing.

❦

So you're the greatest little bargain hunter in the world! Great! But temper your dollar-saving drive when you dive into the great mound of terry towels on sale. Call yourself to one side, housedoll, and recollect the feeling of emerging from the shower and trying to sop up the H_2O with a thin, sleazy towel. Awful, isn't it? And this should add balm to your little penny-pinching heart. The expensive towel will be a savings in the long run. They last longer; they retain their good looks through many a laundering; and they're such a joy to use. Hold each towel up to the light. If you can see through it don't buy it. The thicker a towel, the thirstier it is. Do check with the dealer on the nonshrink qualities, especially of the borders. Puckering up when you want your goodnight kiss is okay for you, luv. It's a very unbecoming activity for your bath towels!

❦

Be a feeler. A good durable towel should have a firm underweave and dense thick loops. And inspect that border. It should be woven loosely or it'll pucker when you launder it. Pastel towels, if they are colorfast, can be washed with your white items. Deep-colored towels should be washed separately.

❦

Don't try to carry colors in your mind when you shop for towels. Carry a scrap of the bathroom wallpaper (don't tell me that you don't save swatches of all your wallpapers!) Or if the walls are painted, take a sample of the paint so the towels will match or blend. You can apply a bit of wall paint to the inside of a match book, a popsicle stick, or a tongue depressor (the drugstore has these).

⚜

Petroleum jelly has many household uses as well as medicinal ones. Dabbed on hinges and wheels, it quiets squeaks. It doesn't drip as oil does. Placed on lipstick stains on napkins before washing them, the stains come out. It also often removes white stains on mahogany tables left by wet glasses. Coat your garden equipment with petroleum jelly before storing this fall. It will prevent rust. Cover metal parts of a home aquarium before the tank is filled. The jelly prevents rust and is not injurious to the fish. Dab it on tracks of bureau drawers that stick. Cover paint bristles with it after cleaning them to preserve bristles. It will protect metal trim when you are painting a kitchen cabinet. Use it to lubricate can openers and scissors to make them work better. Nuts and bolts are easier to remove if you cover them with the jelly. Finally, put it on your tennis racket strings before storing. It will prolong their life.

⚜

Use plastic wastebaskets as large, deep plant containers. They are made in round and square shapes and come in pretty colors and designs, and some are footed. The best part is they cost less than two dollars in many stores.

☙❧

Save soap slivers in a box until you collect a sufficient amount. Then place them in a pan, add small amounts of water, and melt them into a firm jelly. Pour the melted soap into cupcake tins and allow them to harden. Finally, carefully remove the soap from the tins. *Voilà*, new bars of soap.

☙❧

Break soap slivers into small pieces and put them into your blender. (A modern blender with a high torque motor will not be harmed by this.) Results: quick dissolving soap power that can be used in washing small clothing items.

☙❧

Why is it that you can throw a burnt match out of the car window and start a forest fire, but you can use a whole box of matches, the entire Sunday newspaper, and a flock of nice dry kindling without being able to start the fire in your fireplace? Obviously, there are some little leprechauns in the chimney who mischievously blow out your every effort. To thwart them, I'll tell you all I have gleaned about whipping up a blazing fire to brighten a dreary, cold Sunday afternoon. Be sure your logs are hardwood. Softwood gives you a very hot flame, but it also produces sparks. Your andirons should be about twelve to sixteen inches apart. Place a Nantucket log between the andirons or under the grate if you have one. What do you mean you don't know what a Nantucket log is? Simply spread several sheets of your newspaper out on the floor. Roll them, corner to corner, into a long slim telescope. Secure by tying a knot in the middle. Voilà! Nantucket log. Okay, on top of the Nantucket log, arrange a crisscross of kindling sticks. Place two logs on top of the kindling. Put the largest log in front, and do not allow the back log to rest against the fireplace. Place a small split log on top of these two logs and put a page of newspaper on top of all the logs and light it to warm the flue. Light the Nantucket log, put your screen in front of the fireplace, sit back and relax and watch the dancing flames!

⋞⋟

If you lose the little white button on a spray can, you may be faced with having to discard half of the contents, since the warning on the can tells you not to puncture it. Simply borrow a similar cap from another spray can. It works beautifully.

⋞⋟

If you do your grocery shopping right after breakfast or luncheon, the grocery bill is lower. There's no temptation to pick up that "extra little goodie" that you really don't need. Food prices are so high these days that we need all the help we can get.

❦

When you can't squeeze any more shampoo out of the tube, just snip the tube in half with scissors. You'll find that there's enough shampoo left for another washing.

❦

Instead of pulling the tab (covering the holes) off a can of cleanser, simply pull it back and expose two holes only. With this method, you get only the amount needed, and none of the cleanser is wasted. When the can is nearly empty, pull off the tab covering completely.

❦

Are you a detergent-waster? Do you pour the detergent into the dish pan, run the hot water, and produce so many suds you can scarcely find the dishes? Put one squirt of detergent on a sponge, wash the dishes with the sponge, and rinse them under the hot water tap. In a small family one squirt washes all the dishes from one meal and leaves enough detergent on the sponge to wipe the sink and the counter tops.

CHAPTER 3

SAVE YOURSELF

Who is it that says most? which can say more
Than this rich praise—that you alone are you?
—William Shakespeare, Sonnet 84

If you streamline your household ship, give a heave-ho to clutter, and organize your tasks; you'll be singing a song of freedom from care. Don't knock yourself out trying to have the cleanest house on the block. Better a housedoll with a warm smile on her face and a little dust under the sofa, than a grumpy dame who dusts the backs of the pictures every day. You deserve those precious moments of enjoyment. Buy a slant board. Place it near your telephone. While you chat, rest on the slant board, feet up, head down. You'll be rejuvenated and ready for the next chore. Take time out in the morning for that extra cup of coffee, and time in the afternoon for a soothing cup of tea. If you're a career doll, allow time for a restful warm bath before starting dinner. Dinner's thirty minutes late? So what! Be good to you. As our friend Bill said at the beginning of the chapter, there's only one you!

❦

Schedule your spring-cleaning chores to save your energy and your sanity. Plan to do no more than one room a day. List everything that has to be done in each room. Decide how many hours a day you are going to work, and stick to it. Nine to two is plenty, with a half-hour break for lunch. At two-o'clock, blow your own whistle, and QUIT. Take a hot bath or shower, rest a bit, get outdoors for a while before tackling dinner preparations. Make a pact with friends and relatives that long telephone conversations are "out" for the duration of spring cleaning.

❦

Stop staring out the window looking at those glorious signs of spring! The sooner you finish the spring cleaning and painting, the sooner you'll get outdoors to enjoy the sunshine. Here's a pretty-pinkie hint. If you don't wear rubber gloves, protect your hands by applying a generous amount of hand lotion before you start your chores. If you are about to paint, rub your fingertips over a bar of soap. The soap will stay under your nails while you are working and can be easily scrubbed out when you are finished, along with any paint or grime you may have gathered.

You can beautify your closet shelves and whittle your waist at the same time. Resist the temptation to climb to the rung of the ladder that allows you to easily smooth out the shelving. Stay on the rung where you must stretch to get into the corners.

I just finished covering our closet shelves with self-adhesive plastic. It's a tough job, and don't let anyone tell you it isn't. But you'll feel better about the whole sticky thing if you know you're also shaping up the old torso. I found that securing the plastic by pulling it over and under each shelf about an inch made for a neater job. Don't try to do a big area with one piece of the stuff, or you're liable to be all stuck together and wrapped for mailing by the time the skipper comes home. It's better when done in small sections. A wall-paper roller is just dreamy for getting rid of air bubbles. But for those really mean ones that won't disappear, just puncture the bulge with a pin and smooth down, and don't forget—stretch, stretch, s-t-r-e-t-c-h. You'll smooth down your own bulges to boot!

Your ironing board is a fine substitute for a slant board. Set the small end on a sturdy box about sixteen inches high.

Here is a way of preventing all those spills on the kitchen floor caused by little furry pets tipping their food and water dishes. Place carpet tiles under the dishes. They absorb the spills, prevent slippage, and can be washed easily.

Do you wear rubber gloves when washing dishes, but have trouble removing the gloves? The hot water causes hands to perspire and sometimes swell a bit. The gloves stick to the skin. Run cold water over your gloved hands before removing the gloves. Off they come in a jiffy.

When driving a nail, skip the ouch department by winding one end of a pipe cleaner around the nail. Hold it in place by the other end and pound away until the nail is almost driven. Then remove the pipe cleaner and finish hammering.

Cut off two fingers from an old pair of rubber gloves and place one on the broom handle and the other on the dust mop handle. Now when you place these items against the wall, they will not fall down.

No more broken fingernails when you clean the grooves of triple-track storm windows with cotton swabs which have been dipped into an ammonia solution. The accumulated dirt disappears like magic.

Sore fingertips from removing aluminum storm windows for cleaning or storage? Use a thimble on one finger of each hand to push the latches. It works very well.

When you soak badly soiled clothes in strong detergent, save your hands by using the potato masher to plunge them up and down.

Blankets generally are folded and piled on top of each other in the linen closet. If you want to remove one from the center of the pile, the rest come tumbling down. Insert a piece of sturdy cardboard (the shirt cardboards from the laundry work well) between each blanket, you can now take out any one of the blankets without disturbing the neatness of the pile. This idea works equally well with sheets. It's especially helpful if your sheets are queen- or king-size.

＊＊＊

When you are rearranging your closets, attach ribbons to each box that is on a high shelf. Secure a label at the end of every ribbon. You can check the contents quickly without having to climb.

＊＊＊

While your dishwasher is doing its duty each morning after breakfast, wash and cream your face. As soon as the dishwasher turns off, open the door and put your face into the steam that comes pouring out. After dinner, load the dishwasher again, but don't turn it on until one hour before bedtime. Then while it's washing the dishes, wash your face. Cream your face again and take your steam facial when the washer stops. Afterward, splash your face with cold water and pat dry.

＊＊＊

On the days you feel lazy, vacuum the rugs, because the more slowly you push that machine, the better job it will do. Three slow strokes (forward and back) over any area should do the trick.

❦

Here is a beauty hint for all new mommies who need to exercise to get their waistlines back into pre-pregnancy measurements. Fold the diapers and whittle your waist at the same time. Place half the diapers on a chair to the left, the other half on a chair to your right. Place a third chair directly in front of you to hold the folded diapers. Each chair should be far enough away so that you must stretch to reach it. Twist to the left as you fold the first diaper, trying to keep your lower torso facing forward. Then stretch and place the diaper on the middle chair. Repeat to the right.

❦

Hey, there, Mommybird, what have you got working for you while you're working for that crew of yours? You clean and cook, and perhaps wash and iron. Great! But no reason why your brood can't have a nice home, good food, and a glamorous mommy, to boot. As soon as you shoo the skipper and the kids out of the nest in the morning, put up your hair in rollers, cleanse your skin, and apply a good moisturizer that will work for your complexion while you're working. Then think tall as you move about the house. Posture, darling, posture! Stand straight and pull in that tumtum! When you make the beds or polish the dining-room table, stretch your arms and upper torso. When you bend down to pick up a scrap, keep the knees straight and bend from the waist. Pretend that you are a ballet dancer as you move about. Every movement will improve your figure, and the whole business of housework will become a beauty program for you. (Gives you a whole new mental attitude about the old tiresome chores.)

❦

As you well know, nothing can ruin the manicure as quickly as that unpleasant job of scouring pans. I've licked the problem by cutting the scouring pad in two, and then firmly grasping one of the pieces with a snap clothespin. You can scour away just as effectively and save wear and tear on the pretty pinkies.

❦

If you have to change a typewriter ribbon just after you've invested in a manicure, slip a plastic sandwich bag over your hands and change the ribbon with no damage to the fresh manicure. Keep extra plastic sandwich bags in your desk drawer just for ribbon-changing time.

❦

You have a handy implement at hand—the coffee-can key. Break off the tip, leaving a two-pronged key and use it to take the hurt from tight earrings. Just place the little key under the earring hinge and bend the clamp back slightly. Bend gently and a little bit at a time so that you don't break the earring.

❦

Color code your family. With your next towel purchase, assign a particular color to each member of your family. Give them their own color paper cup, so it doesn't have to be thrown away with each use. (It doesn't take long for little tykes to run through a pack of paper cups.) Toothbrushes, combs, and cereal bowls can also be identified by color. Sort pajamas and underwear quickly by ironing tiny patches of colored tape on the inside. No more scrapping over toys. You might also purchase toy trucks and kites in colors. This system sure makes for smooth sailing.

❦

The handles of shopping bags can be very hard on your hands. If the bag is heavily loaded, use five-inch lengths of discarded garden hose slit lengthwise to cushion the string handles. This idea works well with the handles of bushel baskets that are used to carry heavy loads.

❦

Take a sponge and a small squeegee into the shower. While you are rinsing, wipe the glass of the shower with the sponge. Then, when you turn off the water, squeegee the glass. No more soap marks to clean.

Carry a stick cologne in the glove compartment of the car. Apply to your wrists for a fragrant, cooling effect.

Here's an idea to save you from extra floor cleaning. Keep a set of plastic bowl covers (large size) in your grocery shopping cart or baby carriage. Slip the covers over the wheels of the cart or carriage and you can wheel the vehicle right into the house. It would be nice if apartment dwellers used this idea; it sure would eliminate those wheel tracks in lobbies.

CHAPTER 4

TOGGERY TIPS

Whenas in silks my Julia goes,
Then, then (methinks) how sweetly flows
That liquefaction of her clothes.
    —Robert Herrick, "Upon Julia's Clothes"

There are few homes in the world with enough closet space, so start now with an organized plan for garment storage. Browse around the notions department of your favorite store. There are miraculous new gimmicks—belt racks that hold twenty belts, and garment bags for handbags and shoes as well as suits and dresses. Multiple skirt and blouse hangers and see-through boxes can hold lingerie, scarves, and gloves if you happen to be short on drawer space. Set up a fall and winter program for cleaning the closets thoroughly. Dispose of anything you have not worn that season and wash or clean winter garments to be stored for the summer, and vice versa. No place to put the storage boxes? Prevail upon your parents, in-laws, or friends to allow you some room in their attics or basements. But please, doll, don't resort to putting those boxes under the bed. They just become a good excuse not to vacuum!

If you save plastic bags from the cleaners (which you know must be kept away from children) to cover your dresses, try my method. Turn the bag upside down. Now insert the dress so the open end is at the top. Gather the open end together and secure it with a tie-band around the hanger's hook. If one tie-band isn't big enough, twist two or three together. There's a dual purpose for this. Any dust from the closet floor will not filter up to your garment, and if the garment slips off the hanger, it will fall into the bag and not on the floor.

Use shaped plastic or wooden hangers for jackets and coats, clamp-type hangers for skirts, and pant-hangers for trousers. The way your clothes hang in your closet will determine the way they hang on you. If you must use wire coat hangers, bind six or eight of them together with tape before you hang a garment on them.

To keep flimsy garments from sliding off hangers, secure them at the shoulders with pin-curl clips.

❧⬦❧

Ask your skipper to install perforated hardboard (the kind that holds hooks) on the inside of your closet door. It's the handiest way ever to hang your purses and belts.

❧⬦❧

How often have you been pushed for time, snatched something out of the closet and donned it only to remember a missing button, a ripped seam, or a loosened hem? Tie red bows on the hooks of five hangers in your closet. When you shed clothing that needs mending, place the garments on these special hangers. When dressing, you know at a glance that the clothing on these hangers are a no-no. Then, when you sort clothes for cleaning and laundering, check the closets and tend to the repairs.

❧⬦❧

Don't forget the old trick of attaching two snap clothespins to the lower bar of a wire coat hanger if you are in need of a hanger for skirts or slacks.

❧⬦❧

Do you take time to adjust garments when you put them on a hanger? It makes a world of difference in the wear and fit of the dress, suit, or coat. Take the extra time to button the garment and zip the zippers so that it hangs properly.

⋙⚜⋘

When you store away woolen coats, suits, and dresses, use an old nylon stocking as a container for moth-balls or moth crystals. Knot the stocking at both ends and then simply hang it over the hanger that holds the garment. It's best to button the garment so that the stocking is hanging inside the coat or dress.

⋙⚜⋘

Here is a safe and useful way to utilize the wire coat hangers and plastic coverings that come from the dry cleaners. Fold the plastic bag several times lengthwise and then insert the hook of the hanger into one end of it. Wrap the entire hanger with the plastic, taping as needed. *Voilà*, a nicely padded hanger! These are especially fine as extra hangers for a summer cottage.

⋙⚜⋘

Most of us do not make full use of our garment bags. There is always extra space left at the bottom. When you pack your summer clothes for the winter, why not store bathing suits, beach towels, shorts, and so forth right on the bag's cardboard floor? In summer, you can use this space to store heavy sweaters, mittens, wool scarves, and caps.

Don't ever, ever put your fur coat in an unventilated plastic bag. Those skins have to breathe, luv. If you must cover it, make a loose garment bag from an old sheet.

If you own a beaded dress, never hang it on a hanger in the way you would an ordinary dress. Sew tapes from the waistband so that you can secure the tapes to the hook of the hanger and relieve the weight that will pull the dress out of shape.

A supply of tissue paper in your closet will find many uses. Place a sheet over the shoulders of light-colored garments to prevent soil. Use it to pad the shoulders of hangers for dresses with fabrics that might be misshapen by the hangers' outer corners. Stuff the toes of shoes with a wadded piece of tissue as soon as you take them off. They'll keep their shapes a lot longer.

Did you ever want to put a garment back into the cleaners' long paper bag? Quite a trick to do it without tearing the bag. Here's how! Insert a belt, buckle-end down, through the small opening in the top of the bag. Hook the hanger holding the garment into the buckle. Pull belt and hanger hook up through the opening. There you are.

In bad weather, plastic bags over those pretty party slippers (secured around the ankle with rubber bands) will get you from one joyous open house to another without ruining your shoes. They'll keep your little tootsies warm, too! I do dislike pulling boots over fancy footwear, don't you? And you will be careful and not slip, won't you?

When cleaning spectator pumps or saddle shoes, tape the edges of the colored leather with transparent tape so the white polish will not touch the color.

When you wear shoes without stockings in the summer the inner soles will always wear out before the shoe itself. Simply trace the shoe on self-adhesive vinyl paper and cut a new inner sole. Press it down inside the shoe, starting at the heel and working forward. You will find that your shoes feel like new and you can wipe them out so easily when they become soiled.

❦

To clean white fabric evening shoes, go over them lightly with a cloth dipped in cleaning fluid. Then rub flour into the material, allow it to remain for several minutes. Brush out with a soft, clean brush.

❦

Keep an old right shoe under the driver's seat in your car. Put it on when you are going to drive. It saves your good shoe from rubbing against the floor mat and wearing out.

❦

If those squeaky shoes of yours awaken your roommate just as you are tippy-toeing in, apply neat's-foot oil or linseed oil to the sole.

❦

When you lose the tip from a shoelace, dip the end of the lace in some colorless nail polish (use colored polish if that's all you have). When dry, the lace will be stiff enough to poke through the hole.

❦

To remove white marks from shoes and galoshes which accumulate from the salt used on streets during a slippery spell, use a solution of half water and half vinegar. Sponge on, and marks leave! This works beautifully on suede shoes, too. Wring out a little sponge in water, dip in vinegar, and dab the suede with short, quick strokes, so that the shoe does not become too wet. Most spots will disappear and the suede will look like new.

❦

Pull plastic bags over your shoes before you don the boots for that November football game, when the frosty wind might tweak your nose and numb your toes. Not only will the boots slide on in an instant, but the plastic acts as insulation to kep your tootsies toasty warm.

❦

Where to put drippy boots and rubbers? Line a good-sized carton inside and out with self-adhesive vinyl covering that comes in so many pretty colors and designs. Visitors just plunk their boots in the box, which

can sit in your front closet. It wipes out with the swish
of a damp cloth.

Baby shampoo will clean and condition leather boots.
With a soft, clean cloth rub a few drops of baby shampoo into several square inches of the leather. Repeat
until you have covered the entire boot. Use the same
cloth to buff the leather to a natural sheen. This gentle
care is equally good for leather bags and suitcases.

A smart editor solved the problem of walking through
high snowdrifts on his way to the office. He made use
of two large plastic garment bags (from the dry cleaners) by placing them over his feet and securing them
to his trousered legs with rubber bands. He then put
on his boots, hiked through the snow, and arrived at
the office with dry unwrinkled trousers.

Soft boots quickly gather dust as they flop over on the
closet floor. By rolling magazines and inserting them
into the legs of the boots, you can hold them erect.
Magazines the size of *Life* are ideal for this.

Save some long cardboard rolls from wrapping paper, aluminum foil, waxed paper, or paper towels, cover them with self-sticking vinyl to match closet shelves, and insert one in each boot. Then snap each pair of boots together at the tops with a snap clothespin.

❧❦☙

Make a habit of washing your hose as soon as you remove them. If the soil and perspiration are removed immediately, the life of your hose or panty hose will be extended considerably.

❧❦☙

You can get some additional wear from panty hose when you get a run. Cut the legs off the panty hose and wear the panty part under slacks and shorts.

❧❦☙

Here is a little scheme for making panty hose last longer. When a run appears in one leg, cut it off below the welt. When the same thing happens to another pair, do the same thing. You'll don two pairs of panties, but have a complete pair of legs. If the salvaged legs are for the same side, just turn one leg inside out. This way, you can get double wear out of your panty hose. Of course, it's important that you buy several

pairs in the same shade in order to be able to inter-
change them.

❦❧

After washing wool socks, wrap them in a Turkish
towel to remove excess moisture. Then hang them
up. They will dry in half the time.

❦❧

Two methods for cleaning white kid gloves. Put three
to four pairs in a large wide-necked jar that has a screw
top. (Mason jars are ideal.) Pour enough cleaning
fluid into the jar to cover the gloves. Allow the gloves
to stay in the fluid for at least three hours. Remove
the gloves from the cleaning fluid, squeeze out excess
fluid, and place them on your hands. Wipe the soil
from the gloves with a dry Turkish towel. Shape them
on your hands and place them on a towel to dry. After
$1\frac{1}{2}$ hours, place the gloves on your hands again, to
soften the leather. Return them to the towel to dry
thoroughly.

These are simple leather glove washing instructions
which, if followed carefully, have proved to be
succcessful:

1. It is easiest to wash the gloves while they are on
   your hands. Wash often; badly soiled gloves will
   sometimes retain stains.
2. Use a small amount of soap (preferably that with
   a lanolin base). Always use cool water.
3. Rinse thoroughly. In the final rinsing remove

gloves from hands and let the water from the tap run inside each glove.

4. Hang, fingers down, with plastic clips. Don't wring the gloves or lay them on a towel, as water will settle on seams and cause streaks.

5. When gloves are dry, gently work them on your hands to shape them to size.

6. If the gloves are longer than wrist length, fold back the cuff while shaping to prevent unwanted stretching.

❧⚜❧

Handle your flour with kid gloves, gals! Here's a great idea that came all the way from Austria. If white kid gloves are lightly soiled, they can be cleaned with plain flour. Rub the flour into the leather thoroughly, and brush away the dirt.

❧⚜❧

Don a pair of soft gloves before putting on hose. It will eliminate many snags and runs and save you countless dollars.

❧⚜❧

Put on a pair of soiled white gloves when you wash your hose—an easy method of obtaining clean covering for all twenty digits.

❧⚜❧

Plastic sandwich bags are just the right size to hold one pair of gloves. The bag keeps them clean, makes them easy to find in the dresser drawer, and they stack perfectly. Keep your scarves in plastic bags as well. If you don't like to clean dresser drawers, this is a good way to keep things neat.

⁓⁂⁓

If you have enough closet space, here's a simple way to store scarves so they won't wrinkle. Use coat hangers with a no-rust coating that are made especially for drip-dry garments. With plastic-clip clothespins, clip the scarves to the hangers. Allow six to each hanger. The scarves will hang in the closet wrinkle-free. Each one is easy to find. No more digging through drawers for a particular scarf. You might hang them in a garment bag so they'll be dust-free.

⁓⁂⁓

Scarves are popular and also expensive. Sort through your husband's tie collection and extract the ties he seldom wears. Rip them open, press them flat, and face them with remnant materials from your sewing basket. You'll have a colorful collection of scarves. Some can be worn as tie belts.

⁓⁂⁓

If your skipper complains that dry cleaning takes the life out of his ties, try doing the job yourself and you'll probably get a promotion in rank on the old household ship. Make a cardboard form that will slip into the tie and hold it taut (one for the front part, another for the back). Use a commercial cleaning fluid and follow the instructions on the can to the letter. For spot removal, try one of the new spray cleaners that dries into a powder. Most department stores carry them.

⚜

Save the cardboard collar reinforcements that come with shirts when they are returned from the laundry and use them for the collars of the blouses and dresses that belong to the females in the family. They keep the collars and necklines in shape as they hang in the closets. This idea is particularly effective for the low turtleneck-type of neckline that always seems to wrinkle right in the front.

⚜

Borrow Junior's white chalk and rub it on the line around Daddy's shirt collar. While the shirt is sitting in the hamper, the grease will be absorbed and the line will disappear when you throw it into the washing machine.

⚜

Even if you have never baked a biscuit, you need baking soda on your shelf. For your jewelry, luv. An old toothbrush dampened and dipped in the powder will bring a shine to all your jewelry, real or phony.

Eliminate a lot of time and trouble by keeping necklaces and long pearls on a man's tie rack. The metal kind with a row of fingerlike spindles works beautifully for hanging chain belts, hair ribbons, and necklaces. It's a lot easier than searching through a jumbled drawer only to find that the necklace or belt you want is tangled.

A plastic ice-cube tray is perfect as a container for rings and earrings.

Gather several strips of nylon net together and tie them to form a small ball. It becomes a great little gimmick to remove lint from clothing. It costs pennies and works better than most clothes brushes.

To brush a dark wool suit or coat with stubborn lint flecks, dip the tip of a whisk broom in a warm vinegar

and water solution and brush briskly. Shake excess
water from the broom before brushing so you don't
dampen the garment. This method works wonders
with black velvet, too.

❦

After you've lined your shelves with self-adhesive vinyl,
save all the scraps of this material to use to take the
lint off dark clothes. It has much the same effect as
using the sticky side of cellophane tape as a lint remover but the vinyl is easier to handle.

❦

Do you often acquire a felt pen mark on your hand or
arm and are too busy to wash your hands? Try this
trick: A piece of cellophane tape will blot away the
ink stain. You must do it immediately, and often you'll
have to do it several times, but it works.

❦

Get a can of stain-repellent spray that protects upholstery fabrics and use it on new ties. The results are
more than satisfactory. Most spills can be removed
readily.

❦

To protect your maxicoat from slush, spray the hem with stain-repellent spray. You'll find it is much easier to remove the dirt once your coat has been treated.

❦

To keep a dress clean and wrinkle-free for a special evening, step into a plastic cleaner's bag before getting into the car, and sit on it. It protects against dusty car seats, and plastic acts as a buffer against creasing. The bags are excellent in case of rain and will cover the longest formal gown.

❦

Tip to teens: If your prom dress is very fragile, pin that precious corsage to your evening bag. However, if that fellow's feelings might be hurt if you didn't wear it on your gown, protect the material by inserting a little square of felt under the material in the area where the pin goes through. Remove the eraser from a pencil and attach it to the end of the corsage pin so that you don't get stabbed while you're dancing.

❦

What to do with the dress that you just pressed to wear to a party? It gets all squooshed if you put it back into the closet, and hanging it on a shower rod is sometimes precarious (especially in the home of a large family). Buy a commercial doorstop, attach it to the top of the bedroom door, and paint it the same color as the woodwork. It's high enough to hold a long gown and allows the most bouffant dress to billow out until you're ready to put it on.

❧

Don't forget the wonders of the various-sized plastic bags to pack scarfs, gloves, hose, jewelry, cosmetics, shoes, and lingerie.

❧

Now that the domestic airlines no longer care how much your luggage weighs, think how fast we'll be able to pack. No big decisions as to whether to take the blue dress or the yellow dress because it means carting another pair of shoes. Don't forget how much empty space there is in those shoes. As those cagey airlines still limit us to two suitcases, there is still a space problem. But you can enclose jewelry, nylons, gloves, and other small items in those handy plastic bags and shove them into shoes. The luggage that allows you to hang your garments is the greatest boon to travelers since the stagecoach. If you don't have one, try this. Presuming your suitcase is large and you are not trying to take an extenisve wardrobe, pack your dresses (and your fellow's suits) on the hangers, with the dry cleaner's plastic bag over the garment. Your clothes will arrive at the destination practically wrinkle-free! Reason? Because of the hangers, some air circulates between the clothes, and, too, they are all ready to hang in the closet of your chosen away-from-it-all motel!

Travelers should carry a magazine or two. Since there are rarely any pants hangers in motels, a magazine slipped over the bar of a wire coathanger helps keep trousers neat.

If the skipper is taking off for a short trip and needs only one or two ties, use shirt cardboards so they don't wrinkle. Cut three slits in the cardboard and thread the doubled tie through the slits. With this reinforcement, the ties will pack easily and will not shift in the suitcase.

Pack an umbrella at the bottom of your suitcase. "Into every vacation, a little rain must fall!"

Save your skipper's old socks and use them to cover his shoes when you pack them for traveling.

When packing, use layers of plastic rather than tissue between garments to keep them wrinkle-free. Those covers from the dry cleaners will do nicely.

❦

If that good old raincoat goes along with you on your vacation travels, transform the sleeves into carrying cases for your books and magazines. Close the bottom of each sleeve with an oversized safety pin. Stuff the reading material into the sleeves and carry the raincoat over your arm. Of course, I hope you make the plane before it rains.

❦

When packing a white dress, turn it inside out and place it in a plastic bag before you put it in the suitcase.

❦

When packing a suitcase, also use plastic bags to encase shirts. They keep the shirts wrinkle-free and provide protection from dust when you reach your destination.

❦

To keep shirt collars from becoming crushed when traveling, put two pairs of rolled-up socks into the neck of the shirt. This holds the collar firm in the suitcase.

❦

Has Mr. Moth invaded your favorite sweater? Be creative. Use different colored yarns, and work a lazy-daisy stitch around each mothhole—using the mothhole as the pivotal point. Your sweater may become a conversation piece with its original abstract scattered-daisy pattern.

❦

Use a colander to gently squeeze out the water when washing a sweater.

❦

Here's the perfect solution for removing those makeup smudges from your white organdy wedding dress or prom gown. Using just the suds from a mixture of a detergent and water works fairly well, but the ideal remover is a cold-water wool soap. Use the powdered variety, not the liquid soap. Mix it with cold water according to directions on the package. Dip a clean cloth into the mixture, and pat, pat, pat. Then very gently wipe away the smudges.

❦

A slice of bread will often remove makeup smudges from dark clothes.

❦

"Sock it to me with the soda water." That's what you
say to the waiter when he spills coffee on your wool
dress or suit. A clean cloth, a bit of bottled carbonated
water, and some rub-a-dub-dub will save the day and a
cleaner's bill if you act quickly.

❦

If your skipper has been cooped up in a board meeting
with a slew of cigar smokers, his suit probably smells
like a political caucus. Hang the suit on a hanger and
on the shower-curtain rod or someplace near the bathtub. Fill the tub half full of hot water. Empty a
vinegar bottle into the tub. Close the bathroom door
and let the vinegar steam remove the smoky odor.

❦

Here's a tip for your skipper so he won't be a victim of
the overcoat exchange. Unattended cloakrooms in
clubs, restaurants, taverns, and bowling alleys are
responsible for a lot of size 48 fellows ending up with
size 36 overcoats, simply because some preoccupied
gentleman grabbed a garment that looked like his. So
—from my skipper to your skipper—a solution. Button
up your overcoat after you hang it on the hanger or on
a hook. The unthinking character will pause to reflect
as he grabs your coat. Instead of throwing it over
his arm and walking out, he'll realize it is not his. Of
course, if all the skippers start buttoning their over-

coats after hanging them up, they'll be right smack back in the same pickle.

☙ ⛯ ❧

Are the sleeves of your winter coat wide, and does the cold air rush up the sleeves? Solve this problem by using some old stretch knee socks to break the wind. Cut off the feet of the socks, bind the edges, and attach the top of the socks to the lining of the sleeves of the coat.

☙ ⛯ ❧

Use transparent self-adherent wrap around wire coat hangers before hanging wash-and-wear garments. Sleeveless, low-backed dresses cling beautifully to these wrapped hangers. You won't have to bother to bend the hangers or use pins to hold them.

☙ ⛯ ❧

When changing purses, the whole operation can be done in a jiffy if the items in the purse are encased in a plastic bag. Just lift out the bag and transfer from one purse to another.

☙ ⛯ ❧

Part of our code of honor is to not peer into each other's purses. But, being honest with yourself, if someone looked into your purse, would you be proud of the organization of the contents? Someone said that you could judge the orderliness of a woman's mind by checking her pocketbook. I don't believe that for a moment (perhaps I don't want to), but let's call ourselves to one side, gals, and hit on a system for keeping our purses in shipshape order, always ready for inspection!

Keep a plastic drawer divider handy in your bedroom and dump all the contents of your purse into it every evening. Then you can start off each day with a purse that has been brushed and is carrying only the essentials.

❦

This is an effective way to clean those hard-to-get-at places in handbags. Wrap a piece of cellophane or masking tape around your forefinger (sticky side out). You can reach into the corners of the lining and extract remnants of tobacco from cigarettes or particles of dust.

❦

Plastic can keep you warm during the wintry days. Wear a pair of plastic disposable gloves under your regular gloves. Cut a triangle of plastic from a garment bag to place on your head and tie under your chin before putting on a head scarf. You might wear a plastic raincoat under your overcoat. You'll feel as if you were encased in an electric blanket no matter how cold it is.

One way to zip your own back zipper is to use a long piece of strong string. Tie a small safety pin to the end of the string and insert the safety pin into the small hole of the zipper's pull-up. Put on your dress, hold onto the string, and pull the string over your shoulder and—zip! You're zipped.

The line of demarcation from a let-out hem will often disappear if rubbed with a vinegar-water solution.

Keep a plastic bag in your purse to cover your newspaper. This keeps the arms of your light-colored outer garments from becoming soiled by the print.

CHAPTER 5

SEW SHALL YE REAP

A stitch in time saves nine
—Proverb

Forty-four million smart chickadees in the United States sew, and a goodly number of these gals make their own clothes. What with the cost of fine ready-to-wear, it's no wonder that so many fashion-conscious femmes have turned their creative talents toward the sewing machine.

Whether you whip up wardrobes for the entire family or just stick to the mending and button-sewing routine, here are some sewing steers. So, sew, already!

Does your sewing machine jam on the first few stitches? You didn't start properly, baby. Begin with

the needle at its highest point. Hold the ends of the
thread to the back for the first few stitches. Pushing
or pulling the fabric is a no-no.

Stitch through a piece of sandpaper to sharpen the
needle on your machine.

Store buttons in plastic pill bottles.

You may have attended a park-in, a love-in, a zonk-in,
a fun-in, or a weekend-in, but have you ever had a
sewing bee-in? Have all your pals bring their scraps
and remnants. Cut and sew as you drink coffee and
chat. In one afternoon you can whip up a smashingly
new old-fashioned patchwork quilt for the new bride
in your circle.

A little wad of cotton stuck into your thimble will become a fine place to stick your needle before replacing
it in the sewing basket. Easy to find.

Keep two 4-by-6-inch pieces of either paper or cloth in your sewing basket, one piece white and the other black. When threading a needle with white thread, hold both the needle and thread against the black cloth or paper, and vice versa. It's so much easier to see and saves a lot of time. This system is also very helpful when threading a sewing machine needle.

If you still have trouble threading your needle, a little bottle of colorless nail polish in your sewing basket will help you accomplish the task. Dip the tip of the thread in the polish. It will dry quickly and you can thread the needle with ease.

Spray a bit of hair spray on your finger when threading a needle and apply it to the end of the thread. The thread stiffens just enough to ease the job of finding the needle's eye.

After oiling the sewing machine, stitch through a blotter several times. It takes up any surplus oil that otherwise might be transferred to the material.

An easy and fun way to make pillows. Drapery departments often sell pieces of fabric samples. The price is usually very low. Buy these and stitch two pieces together on three sides. (They are more interesting if they don't match.) This becomes a bag to hold discarded nylons. Cut the nylons into pieces and insert them into the bag. When there is sufficient stuffing, sew up the fourth side. A new throw pillow.

Love to sew, but no space for a sewing room? Buy a ten-shelf shoebag—not the pocket type but the kind where the shoes or purses can be placed on the shelves. Put each pattern plus its material and pieces on a different shelf. Every project can be kept separate and clean, since this type of hanging bag has a zippered closing. It's hung out of the way in a closet and is a great solution for neatniks.

Plastic shoe boxes are also good containers for sewing equipment because they stack so well. Use one for pins, needles, and scissors; another for zippers; and others for buttons, snaps, hooks and eyes, elastic and upholstery cords, measuring tapes and rulers, seam binding and patterns. The patterns can be sorted as easily as index cards and readily seen.

A small, deep, fishing tackle box makes an ideal sewing box. The top opens to double compartments to hold spools of thread, needles, thimbles, and buttons. The bottom is deep enough for the larger spools of thread, scissors, patches, and other sewing needs. You can carry it easily without danger of spilling the contents.

When dyeing curtains or a garment, wind thread loosely around a piece of plastic, and dye that at the same time. Then you'll never have to shop around for matching thread at mending time. Cut the plastic from a detergent or bleach bottle and make several ridges in it so the thread doesn't slide off.

Slippery, clinging materials are so fashionable, but have you ever tried to mend a rip in a silk or synthetic jersey garment? It's very frustrating when the material keeps sliding out of your hand. Use embroidery hoops. They keep the material taut, and even an L-shaped rip can be mended in a jiffy.

Behind in your mending? Place the sewing basket and garments to be fixed beside your telephone. You won't feel nearly as guilty about the time you spend

chatting with your pals if you're sewing rips and securing buttons as you gossip.

Attach a small pincushion to a wristlet of elastic.
You'll find it very handy to use when you're pinning
up a hem for a friend.

A razor blade in the sewing basket is a must, but please
don't leave it laying around loose. Remove the matches
from a book and insert the razor blade. Close the
cover and you have a fine protective packaging for the
blade.

Use dental floss instead of thread when sewing buttons
on children's play jackets. It's stronger and will last
through lots of tugging.

Keep a supply of white shirt buttons plus a needle and
a spool of thread in an empty adhesive bandage can.
You can tuck this into a kitchen cabinet. When the
men in the family come into the kitchen in the
morning moaning about a button that has popped, you

can reach for the little can and not have to rummage through your sewing basket.

❦

Secure the buttons of a new garment with transparent nail polish. Lightly coat the threads at the center of each button with the polish. The threads will not unravel. (This is especially good for men's shirts.)

❦

Whenever you make a dress with buttons covered by the material, cover an extra button and sew it to the inside side seam of the dress. It is always available if a button is lost or frayed, and if the garment fades with washing or cleaning, so will the extra button.

❦

Are unused pieces of embroidery thread making a shambles of your sewing basket? Wind the leftover thread around a tie-band that comes with packaged plastic bags and bend the two ends of the band to secure it.

❦

There isn't a housewife who hasn't discovered that the bathroom rug wears out while the matching seat cover is as good as new. It seems a shame to dispose of the seat cover, so double the cover and sew it together to form a giant mitt. Wow! You'll hear the raves from the car washers in your family. No more bruised knuckles. The mitt holds the soap beautifully and does an excellent cleaning job.

If your contour sheet wears thin in the middle, stitch a flat mattress pad to it, and you'll have a contour, nonslip pad.

Glue a tape measure to the area immediately in front of your sewing machine for handy reference.

When sewing snaps on clothes, first sew on the portion of the snap that has a point. Rub a bit of chalk on the point and press into the material. You'll have exactly the right positioning for the other part of the snap.

Dampen and press with a very hot iron all new material that is washable before cutting and sewing. This is a lot of work but it sure prevents shrinkage problems.

CHAPTER 6

LAUNDRY LIFTS

Out, damned spot! Out, I say!
—William Shakespeare, *Macbeth*

Just to put you in a better mood for the washing-ironing chores, let's shift our time gears into reverse and consider doing the family wash in the nineteenth century. Ready? Okay. Here we go. After you've made the soap from lye and grease, you can tote the water from the well and heat it in heavy tubs on the wood stove. Now, sort the clothes and boil the white pieces. Then, scrub each item on a washboard. Wring, rinse, wring again, and immerse some pieces in starch water or bluing. Tired? You can't be. You must make it to the backyard to hang the wash. The next day will be easier. You will heat the flat irons on the stove and reheat them each time they cool. Want to shift into high gear and return to the present day with its automatic washer and dryer? So, smile already, as you set that cycle. You're touching the women's liberator of the century.

❦

When carrying clean clothes from the laundry room to the bedroom, do you take too much and end up dropping things? This means wasted time in refolding. Buy several plastic dish pans in various colors. Stack clothes for each part of the house in its own pan.

❦

Keep a beer can opener in your laundry room. It provides the easy way to open boxes of detergent. Just puncture the top of the box with the pointed end. It saves temper and fingernails.

❦

Whenever you buy an upholstered piece of furniture, a new bedspread, or draperies, ask about the fabric's fiber content. Mark the statistics down on a card (for example: bedspread—84 percent cotton, 16 percent rayon). File the card in your household file. (You do have one, don't you?) Comes the day the puppy jumps on the bed or Uncle Charlie spills the spaghetti sauce on the dining-room chair, you'll know how to treat the spots. Even if the material has been treated with a stain-resistant spray, you still have to know fiber content to attack stains.

❦

Keep embroidery hoops in the laundry room. When pretreating stains, stretch the fabric in the hoops. When material is held taut in this fashion, it is much easier to remove spots.

❦

Mustard is great on hot dogs, but it's pretty unbecoming on the front of your dress. Use glycerin to remove the mustard spot from washable materials. Work it in well and then launder.

❦

Don't cry over spilled gravy. If the material is washable, soak it in cold water. This will dissolve the starch. Then wash. If the spot remains after laundering, sponge it with cleaning fluid. If the waiter spills gravy on your fellow's suit, sponge the stain with cool water immediately. Then when you get home, sponge again with cleaning fluid.

❦

"Heavens to Betsy, Betsy, stop wiping your lipstick off on my good napkin." Have you ever wanted to say it? Of course you have. But one can't go around losing friends over a napkin, can one? So save your temper and your pretty napkins by keeping a commercial lipstick remover on hand. As soon as your guests depart, attack the lipstick stains with this dry cleaner before—and do listen to me, mateys—b-e-f-o-r-e you wash the napkins. Once you plunk them in hot water, you're a cooked cooky. The stain sets. Don't say I didn't tell you!

❦

Here's an authentic solution to that long-time nemesis, the ball-point ink stain. From the American Institute of Laundering comes this happy news. Are you ready? "Hairspray, applied to a ball-point ink stain and allowed to dry before laundering, effectively removes the formerly unyielding blemish." How about that! The laboratory technicians recommend that any surface ink should first be scraped from the fabric, followed by saturation treatment of the stain with hairspray. After the spray has dried, the fabric may be hand- or machine-washed in a conventional manner. If any stain remains, the process should be repeated.

❦

If someone spills red wine on your best tablecloth, shake the salt shaker instead of the poor embarrassed fellow who did it. Sprinkle the spill generously. Remove the cloth as soon as possible (let the guests have their dessert—the salt will save the cloth and your sanity). Dunk it into cold water and rub the stain out before washing.

☙⚬❧

Boiling water poured from a height of several feet through the stain will remove the juice of most fruits from materials.

☙⚬❧

Ever put a load of wash through the washing and drying cycles before discovering a crayon had been left in the pocket of one of your child's garments? Saturate the spots with a hair shampoo and work it in with a brush. The results are amazing.

☙⚬❧

Clean the spots from your good tablecloth as soon as possible. The minute the guests leave, dash for a bottle of the detergent that you use for washing dishes. Dilute it with a little water, and rub into stubborn spots. Allow this to dry, and your spots should disappear with regular laundering.

☙⚬❧

I'm sure you know wax can be removed from tablecloths and most materials by placing a blotter over the waxed area and pressing with a warm iron. In these days of ball-point pens, however, blotters are not that easy to come by. Fold a facial tissue into four thicknesses, and it will substitute nicely for the blotter.

❦

Did the Christmas candles drip all over your good tablecloth? Did the mark persist after you had scraped away the wax and washed the cloth? Try dabbing turpentine on the spot and launder again.

❦

Forever hunting for socks and sometimes losing a few in the washing process? Use very large safety pins and pin three pairs of socks to each pin. Do the same with washable slippers.

❦

Here's an ironing trick learned from an expert. When pressing a Madeira tablecloth or any cloth with heavy embroidery, place a terry towel on the ironing board. Cover the towel with a piece of linen. Then press the tablecloth on the wrong side with a steam iron.

❦

When ironing large articles, such as curtains and tablecloths, fold a large bath towel in half, lengthwise.

Pin each end of the towel to the front edge of the ironing board, hammock fashion. Place your dampened article in this hammock. It will keep it from drying out as well as prevent it from being underfoot.

❦

When storing tablecloths or sheets after ironing, fold them crosswise instead of lengthwise for a change. They'll last longer.

❦

Old terry-cloth towels provide some of the best cleaning rags. They're great for polishing silver and furniture and scrubbing walls. Keep a supply of these worn towels in your laundry room to balance the load in the automatic washer. When you do "odd" articles such as delicates, woolens, etc., throw in a couple of towels. They also act as buffers when washing plastic shower curtains in the washer and drying acrylic blankets automatically.

❦

When washing baby clothes in a washing machine, place the socks and shoestrings in an old nylon stocking, tie a knot at the top, and put it in the machine. It saves many a precious minute.

❦

Delicate colors will not fade as rapidly if you add one teaspoon of epsom salts to each gallon of washing and rinsing water.

❧✦❧

After laundering permanent press white shirts, which are subjected to hard wear, allow them to dry thoroughly and then spray their fronts with spray starch. Let the starch dry thoroughly before wearing. This acts as a dirt repellent on the permanent press material.

❧✦❧

A super way to use those slivers of soap right up to the last smidgen. Cut coarse nylon net into eight-inch squares, place two pieces together for double thickness, put several slivers of soap in the center, and gather the netting around the soap. Secure this packet with a piece of string or dental floss. It's a neat little pouch to keep in the laundry room for pretreating soiled collars on shirts or blouses before they are dunked into the washer. The nylon acts as a scrubber, and the soap slivers give off a rich lather immediately when dampened.

❧✦❧

Ironing shirts? If the sleeve is pressed flat with the cuff unbuttoned, it is easier to press the sleeve neatly. You can do a much more professional job that way.

❧✦❧

Rhinestone buttons? Hesitate about washing without removing them from the garment? Cover the buttons with aluminum foil and carefully wash and rinse by hand. The garment comes out beautifully as long as the water isn't too hot and parts of the button aren't glued together. Sure saves sewing time!

❦

When removing buttons from a garment, protect the fabric by slipping a thin comb between the button and the material. You can then snip away with a razor or scissors.

❦

Grandmothers are the nicest people, but sometimes they buy children's apparel that is difficult to launder —for example, a white overblouse with bright red and blue buttons. Visualize the streaks of color that could ruin the blouse if buttons weren't removed. Put a strip of adhesive plastic wrap over all the buttons and secure each button with a tight rubber band. The blouse can then be washed in the washing machine.

❦

You can starch organdy collars and cuffs with the water in which rice has been cooked.

❦

If your skipper doesn't like starch in his collars but still resents being "wilted" on those hot days, try using a spray sizing that puts the body back into his shirts without making them stiff.

❦

A tip about laundering terry towels: A fabric softener in the final rinse gives towels that luxurious "roughing-it-at-the-Ritz" fluffiness. But don't overdo a good thing. Read the instructions, luv. Too little does no good at all and too much decreases the towel's blotting power. Harken to these words, young mommybird. If you use too much softener on baby's diapers, they won't do their job, either. Just think what might happen when dear elegant Aunt Susie holds the baby. Don't say I didn't warn you.

❦

Add a few drops of your favorite cologne to the rinse water when hand-laundering your lingerie.

❦

The fastidious femme will sprinkle a bit of cologne on her ironing board before pressing lingerie.

❦

"Hem" the ribbon on your lingerie by applying color-less nail polish to the cut edge. The ribbon will not ravel when you wash the garment.

❦

To prevent bra straps from twisting and cutting, spray with spray starch and iron them. The stiffness is wonderful and holds up until the next washing. This is especially good for wide straps worn by heavier women.

❦

Ironing day can be your beauty day. Don't raise your eyebrows in doubt, luv. Just listen carefully: Before you tackle that heap of unironed clothes, cleanse your face and neck thoroughly with soap and water or your favorite cleansing cream. Apply a thick coating of moisture cream to your skin. The steam from the iron will help the cream penetrate every little pore. Think of it this way: The more ironing you have to do, the more effective will be your beauty treatment. Concentrate on improving your posture as you iron. Lift your rib cage high, and pull in the tummy muscles and the fanny. Don't lock your knees. Allow them to bend just a wee bit. You can delay that tired feeling if you keep a footstool under the ironing board. Change feet on the footstool at regular intervals. There's a groovy adjustable stool used by guitar players that you can find in music stores. So ahoy, matey.

Chase away the wrinkles in his shirts and your face all in one fell swoop.

❧❦☙

Be sure you have a firm, well-padded ironing board. Covers come in three sizes: 48, 54, and 60 inches. Buy a plastic sheet to cover the floor area to protect large pieces from soil. When you dampen clothes, use warm water and fold rather than roll them in order to distribute the moisture evenly. Iron low-heat fabrics first and then go on to cotton and linen temperatures. (This prevents scorching.) If you're brave enough to attempt doing shirts yourself, iron in this order: cuffs, collar, sleeves, back, and front. (Personally, I suggest you arrange the budget so the shirts go to the laundry, or else convert him to the wonderful wash 'n' wear shirts.) You can easily iron three handkerchiefs at once.

❧❦☙

Keep the top of that can that held the ham. It's just the right shape to become an iron rest. Tape the edges so that you don't cut your pretty pinkies when you're ironing.

❧❦☙

A plastic catsup dispenser filled with water fills your steam iron in a jiffy. "If the flow is slow, snip the tip."

How's that for adding a little poetry to your ironing?

✦❦✦

Stop guessing how much water to use every time you fill your steam iron. Mark your glass measuring cup with nail polish, designating just how far you will fill it each time that you fill the iron.

✦❦✦

A dampened cloth dipped into baking soda will clean the bottom of an iron. If the iron is very sticky, pour salt onto a piece of brown paper, and run the iron over it. Then "iron" a piece of waxed paper, and your iron will slide like a ballplayer going for home.

✦❦✦

It is quite annoying when starch sticks to your iron. Sometimes, not knowing it is there, it is transferred to a part of a shirt that you don't want starched. I use ooo (triple-o) steel wool to clean the bottom of my iron. Put the steel wool on paper toweling to catch the steel dust. Run the hot iron over the steel wool.

This same type of steel wool has so many uses. It will remove many spots from chrome. I use it to shine the cooking burners of my electric range. It also cleans brass (unlacquered variety) without scratching.

✦❦✦

Triple-o steel wool will rejuvenate old vinyl floors. The vinyl in our kitchen is ten years old, still good, but had lost its oomph. We went over the entire floor with good old triple-o—and *voilà!* even the pretty colors reappeared.

❦

If an iron is not too badly clogged, you may be able to clean it yourself by using three tablespoons of vinegar along with the required amount of water. Turn the iron on high and steam it out as much as possible, tipping it at times to promote the steaming. Refill with fresh water and repeat. Then empty out all the water. If pieces of calcification continue to come out, seek professional care by taking it to an appliance store.

❦

Ironing with a steam iron is faster and easier if you keep the steam holes clean. Dip a pipe cleaner in a solution of detergent and water and insert it into each hole.

❦

Don't you believe that jazz about using dehumidifier water for your electric iron. Distilled water is still the best to keep your iron in good shape, even though the instructions may say you can use tap water.

❦

When ironing an embroidered article, press on the wrong side on a terry-cloth towel. The raised embroidery will sink into the towel, and the flat surfaces can be ironed out smoothly.

❦

Use the small end of the ironing board to press shirt-back yokes. It also works for blouses, boys' shirts, and little girls' jackets.

❦

If that mean old iron of yours went haywire and scorched the skipper's best shirt, run for the peroxide, darlin'. No, not so that he won't recognize you as a blonde. You use the peroxide to sponge the scorched area on the shirt. Then let it dry in the sun, if possible, and launder in hot suds.

❦

After sprinkling clothes to be ironed, place the sprinkled clothes in a Styrofoam cooler. The next day, the clothes will be still damp enough for ironing.

❦

Doing little girls' pretty dresses with puffy sleeves can be a problem. Many of these garments are permanently pressed, but some need careful ironing. A small travel iron does a much better job than a regular iron because of its size.

⚜

A towel bar on the ceiling may sound strange to you, but when it is on a basement ceiling, which is low, and near an ironing board, it is a very handy gadget for holding hangers with freshly ironed garments. Also use it for drip-drys and for drippy raincoats.

⚜

Nothing will make ironing a joy, but there is a method that makes the chore a bit more pleasant. When ironing dresses, mix a few drops of a summer cologne with the water in the steam iron. A few drops won't discolor the garment, but just enough scent is left to make it smell nicely when it's hung in the closet. It makes ironing a fragrant chore.

⚜

Why not iron pillowcases, sheets, and tablecloths on your dining-room table? Use protection pads, of course, and place a large quilt over them. You'll iron a pillowcase quickly, and the tablecloths and sheets don't drag on the floor. The ironing goes so much faster.

⚜

Spend less time on ironing and yet never put an un-ironed sheet on the beds? Oh, c'mon, Dorsey, you've got to be kidding! No, siree! With all the fine ironing hints I've received, I learned that no more time has to be expended on sprinkling, and sheets can be ironed in a jiffy! You know about placing your clean laundry in a plastic bag in the fridge until you are ready to iron it? Well, here's the twist. Put a half-cup to a cup of water in the plastic bag with the clean, dry clothes. Place in the fridge overnight. Everything will be dampened and ready for ironing in the morning. The material absorbs the moisture. No sprinkling! And that's an easy way to iron sheets.

Ironing dust ruffles, and want to keep the material already ironed from becoming wrinkled again? Make folds as you iron and clip the ruffles about every eighteen inches with a large spring-type clothespin.

When ironing large, wide pieces (sheets, curtains, or tablecloths), turn the ironing board around, using the pointed end for resting the iron. This leaves a much larger, rectangular surface to use for ironing those large pieces.

If you don't own a sleeve board for ironing, you can improvise one by rolling a magazine into a cylinder. Cover it with a terry-cloth towel. Use safety pins to secure the towel at the ends.

A clean fly swatter is a good clothes sprinkler (never overdoes the job).

Though you may consider yourself a flopperoo in the sketching department, please make like an artist when you wash your good wool sweaters. Sketch an outline of the sweaters on wide brown paper before you dunk them in the suds. That's the only way to be sure they will turn out the way they went in. Cut out the paper pattern. Use cold-water soap and follow manufacturers' directions. But of course you always read directions, don't you? Work suds throughout the garments without rubbing or twisting, and support each sweater with your hands when squeezing out the water so the weight of the water will not stretch the garment. After rinsing, roll each sweater in a terry-cloth towel to absorb most of the moisture. Then spread out on a flat surface on a dry terry-cloth towel. Shape each one according to its paper pattern and allow to dry away from sunlight and heat.

After you have used your automatic washing machine to dye clothes, run a "load" without clothes and add a little borax to the water to eliminate color that might be left in the machine.

Don't overdo a good thing with that nice new automatic dryer. Overdrying can cause wrinkles and shrinkage. Keep the drying-time chart handy and consult it often. You can dry T-shirts and knit underwear with towels; however, remember to remove the shirts and underwear after twenty minutes and allow the towels to continue tumbling. And watch that lint trap. Empty it after each use. Excess lint in the trap can cause overheating.

Here is the method to use to remove wrinkles from things that have been left in the dryer too long. Dampen a terry-cloth towel (not dripping but just wet) and place it in the automatic dryer with the garments. Turn it on for just three or four minutes. The clothes come out wrinkle-free.

Never dry-clean an electric blanket. Before washing, protect the plug by tying a cloth around it and basting the cloth to the blanket. Spot-clean any stains by rubbing a bit of liquid detergent into the blanket before you put it in the washing machine. Wash on gentle agitation for 1½ minutes. Stop the machine and allow the blanket to soak for 15 minutes. Follow with a fast spin and two regular rinses. Use fabric softener in the final rinse. Spin-dry, using several bath towels as buffers along with the blanket. If you've never known the joy of slipping into a bed warmed by an electric blanket on a cold night, you'd better start bugging your skipper to buy one for you!

Many nylon stockings will last for at least a year with an investment of one dollar in a pair of thin white nylon gloves. Don these when washing hose. Wash the nylons in warm, never hot, water, and use a mild soap. Squeeze, never rub. Rinse thoroughly in warm water, and then roll in a bath towel. Allow them to remain in the towel for at least an hour, and they'll dry quickly when hung on a smooth rack. Wear the same gloves when you put on the stockings and always buy at least three pairs of one kind and color.

Does the thought of washing your lampshades scare you out of your wits? Look, doll, take your courage and your lampshade in your hands. Check to see if the trim is sewed. If it's glued, forget it! But if the material is silk or a good synthetic, you're in business. Whip up a good suds of a few inches of lukewarm water and mild soapflakes in the bathtub. Test a small section of the shade first to be sure it's a washable material. If so, full steam ahead, matey. Wash her down with the suds and a very soft brush. Then rinse gently with warm to cool water. String two lines over the tub and let the shade rest and drip supported by the two lines.

❧⟡☙

Blot your drip-dry Dacron curtains with terry-cloth towels to remove moisture after washing. Wringing of any kind will cause wrinkles.

❧⟡☙

Because of the dust that gathers on curtains or any material, soak them for fifteen minutes or longer in cold water before washing.

❧⟡☙

After washing fiber-glass curtains, fold each panel into pleats and secure the ends with trouser hangers. Hang them with the hem side up for the first half hour and then reverse them until they are dry. The pleats will look as if they had been done professionally. The longer you let them dry, the better the pleats.

❧⟡☙

Mildewed shower curtains might have a second chance. Brush off the mildewed spots as best you can. Then wash in a gallon of water to which you have added half a cup of chlorine bleach and a small amount of detergent. One quick run through your automatic washer and you may salvage the curtains. Adjust the controls for a shortened cycle. Tumble-dry without heat. This same system will also work for plastic curtains, kitchen appliance covers, and plastic storage bags.

A true and tried method of washing shower curtains: Put the shower curtains in a washing machine with warm water and two bath towels. Run through entire cycle. Then rinse by hand in plain warm water to which has been added at least one cup of vinegar. Do not rinse out vinegar. Don't spin-dry. This will cause wrinkles in some types of shower curtains. When finished, the curtains look brand-new and wrinkle-free. This method won't work without the towels, so don't forget them. There are some varieties of fancy hand-painted shower curtains that must be done by hand, but this method is great for most.

To avoid tedious hand-laundering of white shoelaces, string them through the buttonholes of a garment before placing it in your automatic washer. Tie them, and they won't get lost.

CHAPTER 7

HOUSEWORK—YU-U-U-U-U-UCHH!

I cleaned the windows and I swept the floor,
And I polished up the handle of the big front door.
I polished up that handle so carefullee,
That now I am the ruler of the Queen's Navee.
　　　　　　　—W. S. Gilbert, *H.M.S. Pinafore*

You'll find it a lot easier and more enjoyable to put
your H.M.S. *Pinafore* in ship-shape order if you remember that many of your household chores will not
only streamline your household ship but will improve
your figure as well.

Not for one minute am I going to try to tell you that
housecleaning is fun. It's always a pain in the neck,
but I've found one way to ease the pain a bit. Remember as you're scrubbing and polishing that housework is great for your figure, if you do it the right way.
When you lift a chair or a heavy box, bend the knees
slightly, straighten the spine, pull in the tum-tum.
When you make the bed, reach and stretch. Pretend
that you're a ballerina and do a few little knee bends

just before you put on the spread. When you scrub the floor, pull the tummy muscles in until they almost touch your backbone. Relax and repeat. Result: clean floor and one less little bulge around your middle. As you move from room to room, don't walk, JOG! Experts tell us that it is the best exercise of all. And breathe, dolls, breathe! Not just your old unconscious breathing, but nice deep breaths that you hold for a count of ten and then exhale slowly and completely. With all of this going for you, you'll soon find yourself sliding into a smaller dress size.

⋘⋙

My mother always said that you really could clean the whole house with ammonia and water if need be. Her formula is ⅓ cup of ammonia to 1 gallon of water for general cleaning, ½ cup ammonia to 1 gallon of water for heavier cleaning (grease-cutting, spot-cleaning, window-washing, etc.).

⋘⋙

Flocks of smokers coming to your holiday party? Think how that smoky odor will cling to your draperies and furniture. Vinegar will alleviate a good deal of it. Place small decorative bowls or vases on shelves and tables. Fill them with ordinary vinegar before the party begins.

⋘⋙

If it's necessary to head the clean-up committee after a party don't forget the old trick of attaching a paper bag to a spring-type trouser hanger. Hang it on a doorknob to use as a receptacle when you empty ash trays.

❦

Keep a large coffee can with cover in a place handy to the living room. Then, on those evenings when guests have stayed too long, you can collect all the cigarette butts and ashes in the coffee can and put the cover on the can, so smoldering butts can be smothered. You may be too tired to really tidy up the room, but it's very important that those dangerous cigarette butts be removed, and this is the easy way. You can dress up the coffee can, of course, by covering it with an attractively patterned vinyl.

❦

Use pipe cleaners to get between fork tines when polishing silver. They're wonderful for the job. Easy and thorough.

❦

To prevent black spots caused by moisture from forming on clean silver, wrap each piece in paper towels or napkins and then in foil or plastic. The paper absorbs the moisture and keeps the silver bright and spot-free.

❦

Use a fine-pored soft sponge to clean your silver, instead of a cloth. It will penetrate every crevice.

Carbonated water will shine up stainless steel in a jiffy.

Don't try to make your pewterware shine like silver. It's not supposed to gleam. Never use steel wool on it. Just wash with soap and water and polish with a paste made of pumice powder and olive oil, then rinse thoroughly.

Antique copper will be kept bright and shining by cleaning with paste made of salt, flour, and vinegar. Apply this homemade polish with a clean powder puff, wash each item in warm, soapy water, and rinse in clear, warm water. Dry thoroughly.

Use the tarnish-preventive cleaners for silver, copper, and brass. You won't have to polish nearly so often.

For hard-to-clean brass, such as door plates, use a mixture of salt and lemon juice.

◄§§►

Use 70 percent alcohol for cleaning stainless steel sinks. It is an organic solvent and most effective in killing bacteria, too. In using it as a cleaning agent, no rinsing or wiping is necessary and the reason stainless steel often spots is because it is not wiped completely dry. There is a wide price range on this product (called rubbing alcohol in the stores), so shop for a bargain. The price has no effect on the performance of the product.

◄§§►

Do you have a lovely vase or decanter—perhaps a treasured wedding gift—that refuses to look sparkly clean no matter how thoroughly you wash it? Uncooked rice is the answer to your problem! Place some rice in the vase or decanter, add a few tablespoons of vinegar, and shake. Rinse. If the vase is still cloudy, refill with a warm detergent, add more vinegar, and let it soak overnight.

◄§§►

Cut glass will shine and sparkle if you use vinegar in the rinse water after washing. Give a final polish to the piece with soft tissue paper.

◄§§►

After you clean glass, polish it with a paper towel or crumpled newspaper.

⊷⧉⧉⊶

That tedious task of washing all the seldom-used crystal and china can be rewarding if you take the extra time to wrap each item in transparent adherent wrap. Think of the future joy when you take out the precious dishes and glassware and don't have to wash them again before using.

⊷⧉⧉⊶

Dislike the chore of washing good china pieces before using them? Solve the problem by buying large plastic bags used for disposal units. They cover stacks of dishes, as well as such oddly shaped ones as the gravy boat and serving dishes. All are kept dust-free.

⊷⧉⧉⊶

Don't crowd pretty new china on shelves. Stack the plates with two thicknesses of paper towels between each plate. Wrap the spouts and handles of delicate teapots and pitchers with aluminum foil to prevent chipping. Suspend your cups from cup hooks in the cabinet. Wash your china in warm (not boiling) soapy water and place a dish towel in the bottom of the dish pan or sink to protect the dishes. Rinse thoroughly and set on a rubber mat or several thicknesses of paper towels to drain. Don't ever, ever use scouring powder or steel wool on your pretty china. If there are coffee, tea, or other stains, moisten a dishcloth and dip it in baking soda. That will rub the stains away without marring your dishes.

❦

A newspaper will help you clean the inside of a vacuum bottle. Use hot water with detergent or baking soda. Toss in torn bits of newspaper for abrasive action. Shake well. Rinse thoroughly. Place upside down to dry. Then set the bottle upright and leave uncapped until ready for use. Never immerse the entire bottle in water. You may find that moisture will seep into the walls of the vacuum.

❦

You know what a weird odor sponges acquire. Just tuck your sponge in the silverware compartment of the automatic dishwasher. It comes out of the cycle smelling sweet and clean each time.

❦

Draperies in the way when you vacuum? Sew snaps to the inner lower corners. Sew the other part of the snap high enough up on the inside of the drape to give you plenty of room to vacuum when the drapes are snapped up.

❦❦❦

A car snow brush is absolutely the greatest for getting over, under, and into hard-to-reach spots. The handle is long and flat and the bristles are just stiff enough to gather the dirt that clings behind refrigerators and ranges, etc. It's also useful for shorties to reach the back of shelves.

❦❦❦

To simplify the cleaning and dusting of venetian blinds, buy an inexpensive pair of men's white cotton gloves, the kind that have a rather fleecy lining. Turn them inside out, put them on your hands and dust in a jiffy. When they become soiled, just switch the gloves to opposite hands, in order to use the clean undersides.

❦❦❦

Here's a way to clean metal venetian blinds that requires no rinsing and leaves no spots. Saturate a cloth with rubbing alcohol and fold it so it cleans the top and bottom of each slat at the same time. It's quick and easy.

❦❦❦

The rubber plate-and-bowl scraper that resides in your kitchen cabinet drawer can be the handiest little gadget ever for dusting the shutters or venetian blinds. Just cover the scraper with a soft cloth. Because of its pliability, it will reach into every nook and cranny without harming the surface of the shutter or blind.

❦

A little paintbrush is handy for dusting nooks and crannies of china or porcelain ornaments.

❦

Here is a method of cleaning crystal chandeliers that is fast and most effective because it does not require the disassembling of the fixture. The area underneath the chandelier should be protected by newspaper or a drop cloth. Fill a water tumbler with one part alcohol to three parts of water. Now raise the glass up to each pendant until it is immersed. The crystals will drip-dry without leaving water spots, lint, or finger marks. The crystal parts not accessible with a glass should be wiped with the solution. Metal parts should be wiped with a soft dry cloth. No water, as rusting may ensue.

❦

To clean a crystal chandelier, wear cotton work gloves and dip your gloved fingers in ammonia water and clean away. You can do the job in half the time as you work with both hands.

A quick and easy way to remove candle drippings from glass candlesticks is to place them in a container of hot water and add a splash of ammonia. Allow them to soak. Most of the wax will float to the top of the water. Any remaining wax can be removed with a swish of a cloth.

Nylon net removes the wax easily from candle holders and does not scratch the finish. Cut a square of the net and gather the corners to secure them with a rubberband. This forms a net ball which is easy to work with.

If the wax from dripping candles clings to your silver, glass, or metal candlesticks, allow hot water from the tap to run over the candlestick until the wax is pliable enough to be lifted off.

Place candlesticks in the fridge while you do other chores. A few hours later, take them out. The wax will peel off in a jiffy with absolutely no injury to the silver.

❧❦❧

If candles do not fit into holders properly, they can often be adjusted by holding the bottom of each candle in hot water until the wax is pliable and then inserting it into the holder. This takes a little longer than using a match to soften the candle bottom, but there is no danger of dripping.

❧❦❧

When you want clean windows in winter use one-half alcohol, one-half water solution. Your windows will shine like diamonds and no freezing.

❧❦❧

When washing and polishing windows, use vertical strokes on one side and horizontal strokes on the other, so that you'll know which side the streaks are on.

❧❦❧

A length of nylon net makes a great dry cleaner for windows. The net can be used many times before laundering and your windows will always shine.

❧❦❧

A bit of kerosene in the water when you wash the windows will cut the grease and grime in an instant.

❦❦❦

A razor blade is most effective for removing paint from window panes. If you do not have a single-edge blade, protect your fingers by inserting a double-edged blade in the cover of a matchbook. Remove the matches and the soft cardboard first, and the sturdy portion of the matchbook makes an ideal holder for the razor.

❦❦❦

Wax the windowsills after painting them. The dirt will just whisk off.

❦❦❦

Your mirrors will sparkle if you clean them with a piece of cheesecloth soaked in a vinegar-water solution (about one tablespoon to a quart). The same treatment does wonders for windows, too, especially if you then polish the windows with crumpled newspaper.

❦❦❦

Use a vinegar-water solution to wipe vinyl floors between scrubbing-waxing times. It cuts the dirt without removing the wax. Add about a cup of vinegar to a gallon pail of tepid water.

❦

Your mirrors will sparkle if you add bluing to the water when you wash them.

❦

If you're going to the trouble of washing windows, take the time to wash the screens as well. If you don't, the first rainstorm will make your windows just as dirty as they were before.

❦

Use a plastic ball scourer with detergent suds to scrub window screens before storing them. And, pretty please, number each screen with a felt marker pen. Identify the number on a file card so that next spring the screens will go back into the proper windows zim-zam-zoom!

❦

Place a plastic bag over the head of an oiled mop or a dry dust mop before placing it in the utility closet.

It preserves the oil or polish on the mop and protects the other cleaning equipment as well.

Dampen your dustpan instead of your spirits before trying to pick up that little mound of dust. It will adhere.

Give a gal enough rope, and she'll carry all the dust-cloths she needs to clean the whole house. Just tie a rope or heavy twine around your waist and attach sundry cleaning cloths to the rope with snap clothes-pins. Use one of those fine vegetable baskets with a handle to carry all of your cleaning supplies. Mine measures 8 by 19 inches. Flash your false eyelashes at your supermarket manager, and you're a cinch to get the basket for nothing!

The orange stick with the rubber end which is used for manicuring your nails can also help you with your household chores. Wrap a damp cleaning cloth around either end and use it to get into corners of built-in soap dishes, to remove grout around faucets, and to clean the wood corners of frames of French windows.

Buy inexpensive powder puffs to keep in the jars of silver polish and copper cleaner. It's so handy, and you never have to bother looking for a suitable polishing cloth. Keep thin sponges attached to other bottles and cans of household cleaners and secure them with rubber bands or a piece of elastic.

❦

The greatest dishcloth ever is a combination of nylon net and terry cloth. Cut a twelve-inch square of nylon net and then cut a square of colorful terry about a half-inch bigger than the net. Turn the extra half-inch of terry over as a hem. The terry alone is great for washing dishes, and if you need a little scour power, there it is right on the other side of your cloth.

❦

Use your "kitchen sink" toothbrush (any discarded brush will do) to clean parts of a food grinder. It's a must to scrub the indentation of lids of refrigerator dishes and food graters. It does a dandy job around sink faucets.

❦

Favorite shortcutters are the commercially boxed wooden picks with cotton-covered ends. These little rascals will get into unbelievably small areas on the

stove and will scoot down into the gasket on the refrigerator door. You will find them just right for cleaning out accumulated lint from the facings of your
husband's shirts when you are ironing.

❦

Copper sparkles when cleaned with vinegar and salt.
You can also remove dirt and rust from sink and
bathtub mats by letting them soak in a vinegar-and-
water solution before scrubbing them. Too, vinegar in
any rinse water acts as a softener and cuts the soap.
Finally, a hard-to-open glue bottle will stop resisting
if a little vinegar is rubbed into the hardened glue.

❦

Did you ever take dishes out of your dishwasher and
start to put them away, only to discover that they had
not been washed as yet? This happened in our house
so often that we devised a system. We called all of the
crew to attention and announced a new order of the
day. Anyone who empties the dishwasher must immediately fill the washing-powder receptacle. Now we can
tell at a glance whether the dishes in the machine are
clean.

❦

Cover an old lazy susan with self-stick vinyl and
place it under your sink to hold dishwashing ma-

terials. With just a turn of the wrist, you have detergent, soap pads, or cleanser. No more poking into cabinets for the silver cleaner. Everything is handy.

<hr>

Keep a child's toy broom, mop, and dustpan in the enclosed area under the sink. They're handy to clean up minor spills without the necessity of running to the utility room for the larger ones.

<hr>

Rubber gloves too hot? Buy a set of rubber fingers like the ones used in offices. Protect your manicure with these fingers for all scouring and scrubbing jobs.

<hr>

Use aluminum foil on bathroom and kitchen shelves. Ordinary shelf paper is ruined with one spill but foil can be wiped off in a jiffy. Use foil on the shelves under the sink, too. Damp sponges and scouring pads can be placed right on it, with no harm done.

<hr>

Here is a fast and safe way to clean an oven. Place a terry-cloth towel in the bottom of the bathtub and pile all removable parts of the oven on it. Draw enough hot water to just cover the racks, etc. and sprinkle a cup of automatic dishwasher compound over this. While you clean the inside of the oven with the compound and water the other parts are soaking clean.

❦

A wet paper towel sprinkled with automatic-dish-water compound will clean spills from the inside of your oven like a charm.

❦

To scour sinks soak a dish towel with household-bleach and lay it over the bottom of the kitchen sink. In the morning, a quick washing of the sink removes stains, including rust.

❦

White vinegar applied to a stainless steel sink will give it a sheen.

❦

For all those kitchenauts who find waxing the kitchen floor a chore, buy a seven-inch paint roller and pan just for this purpose. It's an easy way to apply the wax. When the job is finished, wash the roller and pan with a mild suds rinse, and it's ready for the next time.

❧⚜❧

Never use water on wood floors. Use special cleaners and wax. Make a nice little cloth cap that fits right over your dust mop for floor polishing.

❧⚜❧

Always rinse a floor thoroughly after scrubbing it. It's a pain in the neck, but it's got to be done, if you want your waxing job to be super. Any soap or detergent residue left on the floor will mix with self-shining, water-base waxes and make them less water-resistant. Also, if you use a sponge mop, never use the same head for applying wax that you have used for scrubbing the floor. No matter how thoroughly you rinse the sponge, some residue from the detergent will remain in it. Be a good girl and put another mop head on your shopping list.

❧⚜❧

The perfect solution to prevent sore knees that you get when you scrub the floor: Use padded knee guards worn to play football. They slip on easily and move right along as you scrub.

❧⚜❧

Stubborn spots and heel marks can be removed from parquet floors with very fine steel wool.

❧❧❧

Use water softener in the cleaning solution when you wash tile. It enhances the cleaning properties of the solution.

❧❧❧

Clean grout (around bathroom and kitchen faucets and tubs) with a toothbrush dipped in a bleach solution.

❧❧❧

Use a toy hand-sweeper cleaning around the carpeting in the bathroom next to basin or toilet, as the area is so small. It doesn't pull the carpeting loose at the edges and does a fine job of picking up threads and loose hair.

❧❧❧

The time to clean the bathroom is when it's still steamy from those morning showers. With a whisk of a cloth, you can shine the glass, mirrors, and tile. You might just place a sign on the door: "Yoo-hoo, you! Close the door to the loo." If the family responds, the steam may be trapped long enough for you to enjoy your second cup of coffee.

❦

Dread cleaning the shower? Instead of using a sponge or cloth with your favorite detergent solution, do the whole job quickly and easily with one of those sponge mops with a little squeeze handle on it. It makes it so simple that you could almost stand outside the shower stall dressed to go out to dinner and clean the shower without getting a drop on yourself. And you don't have to bend down to do any part of the task.

❦

A pencil eraser will remove ugly rust spots on Formica. Use an eraser also to remove rust spots from a ceramic-tile floor.

❦

Nylon rakes for shag carpeting and rugs will help keep them clean. Rake the pile up the wrong way so the shag stands up when you vacuum. This enables you to pick up deeply embedded soil. Then use the rake again after vacuuming to smooth the pile down the right way so it has a pebbly appearance.

❦

To remove marks in the rug caused by heavy furniture's legs, hold a steam iron over the spot—not on the spot, mind you, but about an inch above. Brush the pile up as it steams.

❧

Quick action and an ice cube will remove coffee and cola stains from carpeting of pale shades. Blot the spill immediately with a terry-cloth towel. Then rub an ice cube briskly over the spot.

❧

Remove ball-point pen marks from carpets or upholstery by sponging with sour milk. When the milk is absorbed, apply again until the spot has disappeared. If there is no sour milk in the fridge, make your own by adding a little vinegar to sweet milk.

❧

No matter what Aunt Susie told you, milk is for babies and not for your piano keys. When cleaning the ivories, use a dampened cloth—wrung out almost dry so the water does not run down between the keys—and a mild soap. Rub from the piano toward you. Dry immediately.

❧

Before placing the foam rubber back into sofa covers after washing them, cover the foam with big plastic bags. No more tugging and pulling. They just slide in like a charm.

❧

If you have old-fashioned wooden kitchen cabinets with drawers that stick on the wooden runners, apply floor wax to a clean cloth, pull out the drawers, and run the wax over the runners. Presto, they slide as easy as pie.

❧

You'll find it much easier to put a contour sheet on the mattress if you secure diagonal corners first. For instance, place it over the bottom right-hand corner and then the upper left-hand corner of the mattress. The other two corners will slip into place without a tug.

❧

Here's how to keep your linen cabinet orderly. If you have two different-sized beds and several different colored, striped, and flowered sheets and are always hunting for those that go together, do this. Fold one matching sheet inside the other and the pillow cases inside the sheets, after ironing them. You can reach into the closet and get what you want all in one bundle.

❦

Parchment lamp shades should be conditioned occasionally with a leather conditioner or castor oil to keep them from becoming dry and brittle.

❦

Does your fireplace look grubby? Here's a great way to clean it. Add four ounces of yellow laundry soap to one quart of hot water. Heat until the soap dissolves. Cool it, baby! Stir in one-half pound of powdered pumice and one-half cup of household ammonia. Mix thoroughly. You might have a bit of a problem finding powdered pumice, but usually your local hardware store can order it for you. Now go to work. Remove as much smoky deposit as you can. Apply a coat of the soap mixture with a paint brush. Allow it to remain on the stone or brick for thirty minutes. Scrub it off with a scrubbing brush and warm water. Sponge with plenty of warm water to rinse. *Voilà!* Beautiful fireplace.

❦

Rubbing alcohol will clean the rubber of children's sneakers.

❦

There are many uses for those 9-by-12 foot plastic sheets. When having a dinner party, set the table the day before so you'll have plenty of time for cooking and a bit of relaxing on the day of the party. After setting the table, cover it with the plastic sheet to ward off dust.

❦

Did you know you could wash your records? Use warm water, a mild detergent, and a soft sponge to remove the dust that becomes impacted in the grooves. Rinse under the tap and dry with a lint-free cloth.

❦

Use a pipe cleaner to clean the intricate parts of your sewing machine and your record player.

❦

Rejuvenate your kitchen by applying vinyl wallpaper to all the drawers and shelves. It is easy to handle and washable and the pretty designs really perk up an old kitchen. It is also kind to the pocketbook.

❦

Ever have difficulty cleaning the dial face of the telephone? Cotton swabs do the job in a jiffy.

❦

If you want to do a really thorough job of washing and polishing a light-colored telephone, use masking tape to hold down the shut-off buttons under the hand-piece. You dispense with the dial tone, a call can come through, and you can polish to your heart's content.

❦

When you clean closets, take the time to wax the poles. You'll be happy every time a coat hanger glides along easily. What's more, if the poles are painted, the wax will preserve the finish.

❦

To remove cobwebs from walls and ceilings in seconds without smearing, simply touch the webs lightly with the bristles of a split-tip plastic broom. The cobwebs adhere to the plastic bristles and can be readily wiped off with paper toweling.

❦

When you wash your walls, be sure to dust them down thoroughly first. Use two clean dust-mop heads as gloves to save time and to do a thorough job. Always wash walls from the bottom up. Otherwise streaks of dirty water will run down the sides of the walls and leave permanent streaks. Wash walls in small, circular areas, each circle overlapping the next circle.

What's more annoying than having water trickle down your arm as you wash the ceiling or the walls? Prevent this by folding a washcloth two or three times and wrapping it, bracelet fashion, around your wrist. Secure with a rubber band. It will catch all drips.

An easy way to clean wood louvered doors is to wrap a damp cloth around a plastic bowl scraper. It reaches into every corner.

CHAPTER 8

RISE AND SHINE

I love it, I love it; and who shall dare
To chide me for loving that old armchair?
—Eliza Cook, "The Old Armchair"

The greatest furniture polish that has ever been invented is elbow grease. Not that there aren't some very fine products on the market, but believe me, unless they are applied with vim, vigor, and a bit of affection, they aren't worth a hoot. Polishing the chairs and tables you live with can be very therapeutic, especially when done to music. I'm strongly in favor of every housedoll carrying a portable radio with her as she moves about the house to do her chores. Please try it!

Use a wire coat hanger's curved ends to tuck the slip-covers snugly into the back and sides of the sofa and upholstered chairs. It saves time and fingernails.

Spray a fabric protector on your upholstery fabrics to protect them from spills.

That thin rubberlike material that is sold to put under throw rugs can be used successfully under cushions on wooden benches to keep the cushions from sliding.

Baby oil sometimes removes the white rings which a glass leaves on dark wood. The very same baby oil sometimes works on removing those trouble spots from marble.

Another remedy for the white ring on your pretty table top: Rub white petroleum jelly into the mark and leave it on overnight. If that doesn't do it, rub cigarette ashes mixed with olive oil into the ring, gently please! If the ring is still there after that, better call that fellow who refinishes tables.

Use this method to remove minor scratches from mahogany. It works like a charm. Cover each scratch with a generous smear of white petroleum jelly. Allow it to remain for twenty-four hours, then rub it into the wood. Remove the excess and polish in the usual manner. It sounds unbelievable, but try it.

Scratches on dark wood furniture can often be removed with the meat of a freshly shelled walnut. Rub it on the scratch until the oil of the nut permeates the wood.

Think twice before you invest in a table that has a marble top. Beautiful it is, but it is also highly subject to stains because of its porousness. If you relish the "look" of marble, think in terms of the "trompe-l'oeil" finish that is found on many tables. It's actually paint on wood, and requires little care. However, if Aunt Tillie left you a marble table, you'll be happy to know that there are some fine marble stain removers on the market. Or you can make a thick paste of hot water and scouring powder, wet the stain with hot water and spread the paste over it. Let it stand until it is completely dry (a whole day is often necessary). Use a damp cloth to remove the paste, rinse, and wipe dry.

＊

If the yen to be artistic and the desire to dress up your home is bubbling up inside you, don't be afraid to tackle the refinishing of some cherished piece of furniture. The antiquing kits on the market make the work of a rank amateur look professional. Consult your paint store or department store's paint section. The kit's instructions are explicit. Joyfully enough, you don't have to do a lot of sanding, and the paints come in such luscious colors as avocado or pink, along with antique white. Turn that old chest of Aunt Susie's into something that looks like a collector's item. When I clamored for a new dining-room set, my skipper antiqued our old one, and believe me, I wouldn't part with it now.

＊

In antiquing furniture you may have a problem in refinishing the knobs. It's impossible to handle them and paint them at the same time. And what do you do with them when they're ready to dry? Aha! The plastic coffee-can lid. That does the trick. Insert a hole in the lid's center, and using the original screw, attach each knob to the plastic lid. It is easy to handle the lid as you paint the knob. Then you simply put the lid back on the empty coffee can to let the knob dry.

❦

Try using a small piece of carpeting to work in the glaze when antiquing furniture. It gives a beautiful grained effect.

❦

Use a nutpick for hard-to-get-into corners. Wrap a cloth around the point and you have a perfect dusting instrument for crevices. Dip the wrapped point in detergent water and you can clean the remotest indentation of kitchen cabinets. If you're a paint refinisher, use the nutpick to remove softened paint or varnish from furniture carvings or grooves. For the turned grooves on chair rungs or legs, run a string back and forth.

❦

Save plastic lids and use them under the legs of furniture after shampooing the rugs. Leave them there until the rugs dry. Never a rust spot.

CHAPTER 9

DECOR DELIGHTS

It takes a heap o' living in a house t' make it home.

—Edgar Albert Guest

Most homes have tables, chairs, beds, lamps, but what is it that makes your home the place you want to be? It's you, baby! Not the big hunks of furniture, but your little touches. The colors that make you happy. The pictures that give you a lift. The bric-a-brac that brings pleasant memories to your mind. No decorator can find these things for you! Your home is a mirror. Happy reflections!

Pictures hanging cockeyed drive you up the wall? Wind some adhesive tape around the center of the picture wire. The wire will be less likely to slip on the hanger.

❦

Before hanging a picture, place two small pieces of transparent tape in criss-cross fashion over the spot where the nail is to be inserted. This will prevent cracking of the plaster.

❦

When hanging pictures, a wet fingerprint shows you the exact spot for the hanger. The print dries without a mark.

❦

Are you ruining your walls with experimental holes in attempting to hang pictures and mirrors? Use this system: Cut a paper pattern of each picture and mirror and pin it to the wall, eyeing it for correctness of placement. Find the correct place to put the hanger by using a sharp pencil which perforates the paper to mark the wall.

❦

If you like to change pictures often, think of covering the walls with grass cloth. Nail marks will not show.

❦

A rubber spatula is just great to level off plaster filled-in spots and to clean the excess plaster from each area. Rinse the spatula under the cold water tap before the plaster dries on it.

❦

Unfinished frames can be stained beautifully with ordinary liquid shoe polish. It's so easy to apply with the dauber that comes with the polish. Apply a coat, allow to dry, and then apply another coat. Wax with a paste wax, and the frame has a lovely patina. Brown polish gives the wood a walnut glow, and oxblood polish emulates a rich mahogany. Tan appears as a light maple, and the black is striking.

❦

Did you know a touch of shoe polish in the right shade will often hide a knick on a wood floor? Use the same technique as above and wax after drying.

❦

When installing kitchen carpeting, use reversible tape to secure the seams' edges so the carpeting can be taken up with less bother than if it were tacked.

❦

Save the sticks from the kids' Popsicles. They'll become decorating treasures for matching colors when shopping. When you paint walls, apply some of the paint to the Popsicle stick. It's a handy color guide to slip into your purse.

❧

A quick, easy way to cover small lampshades is to buy curtain valances. Sometimes you can find them on sale for a fraction of their cost. Put drawstrings through both the top and the bottom of the valance and tie it over the lamp shade. After the valance is tied, even out the shirring. When the shirred shades become soiled just untie and it becomes a straight piece of material that is easy to launder.

❧

Sheer white organdy curtains are the prettiest window treatment that you can give to a bedroom. But then your little housewifely heart goes kerplunk when the skipper opens the window at night or turns on the air conditioner. The perfect solution is to sew tiny white bone rings to the bottom inner corners of the curtains. (They're scarcely noticeable.) Then screw little cup hooks into the woodwork of the window frame high enough so that you can hook your precious curtains out of the way of the breezes. Paint the cup hooks the color of the woodwork. This will save a lot of wear and tear on you and your organdy pretties.

❧

By slipping a small plastic sandwich bag over the end of a curtain rod, the rod slides through the hem in a jiffy.

Beaded curtains for a large window are quite expensive. String uncooked *mostaccioli* noodles on strong string and spray them with two coats of enamel. These noodles are cut on an angle and they hang in an interesting zig-zag pattern. Buy a rod made for bead curtains and attach the noodle-bead strings. Alternate colors when hanging the strings of noodles. You might spray half of the strings royal blue and the other half lime-green.

When you send draw draperies to be cleaned for the first time, as you remove the hooks, mark the places where the hooks were inserted with pink nail polish. These dots remain through the cleaning.

If your draperies hang on particular windows, number the panels, starting from left to right. Use colored thread and mark on the wrong side on the bottom hem. No. 1 panel, 1 long stitch; No. 2 panel, 2 long stitches, etc. Be sure to knot the stitches well so that they will remain throughout the cleaning.

For oddly shaped flower containers, make a frog of aluminum foil. Scrunch it up to fit the container, and then poke holes in it with an ice pick.

❦

Buy kitchen curtains longer than necessary. Use the material from the bottom of one to make a toaster cover. The leftover material from the other curtain provides the makings for a mixer cover.

❦

An idea to help decorate an apartment without spending too much money. Buy a tea towel patterned with colorful flowers. Cut it into six segments and frame each in an inexpensive frame. Presto—three darling pictures for the bathroom and three for the kitchen. They also make lovely gifts.

❦

Spray those tired artificial flowers gold for an added touch of luxury decor.

❦

Want to have some of the new "beadangles" to decorate the outside of plain shower curtains and the bathroom window? Save the pull-tabs from cans, and make chains of them. Spray them with paint and hang them from window and shower curtain rods. You'll have a smartly styled bathroom at little cost.

❦

Moving, and the bathroom carpeting doesn't fit the new bathroom? Cut the carpet into two oval rugs, wash them in your washer, and fluff them in the dryer. They'll be beautiful and will go with your color-coordinated bathroom.

❦

For those absent-minded friends who might just walk through your glass sliding-doors, protect them and the doors with pretty butterfly decals.

❦

Household plants usually sulk when moved to a new location or when repotted. Give them time and a little loving care, and they'll perk up in their new surroundings. If all else fails, remember, your bathroom is the closest thing you have to a greenhouse because of its humidity. Besides, it's soothing to view green growing things as you loll in your bath. Makes you feel like a woodland nymph.

❦

Cover the soil in your window boxes with gravel. This will prevent the raindrops from splattering dirt on your windows.

❦

A helpful hint for workshop devotees who are moving: Before removing all those screwdrivers, wrenches, etc., from the pegboard, take a snapshot of the board. When you unpack in your new home, everything can be arranged exactly as before if you use the picture for a guide.

❦

At moving time mattresses might be dragged or dropped. Cover them with two fitted sheets. It's a lot easier to wash the sheets than to try to spot-clean the mattresses.

❦

Buy several packets of different-colored tags. Select a different color for each room of your new house and then tag everything before it is moved. Tag kitchen equipment white; the bedroom, blue; the living room, red; and so on. Make a color chart for the movers, and everything will be placed in the right rooms without your being there. It makes the whole operation smoother and faster. It may also save money for you if your movers are paid by the hour.

❦

Moving day? Instead of packing and wrapping good china plates separately, slip paper plates between them and wrap two or three plates at a time with newspaper. This saves time in packing and unpacking and gives fine protection to the plates.

❦❦❦

It is wise to pack a special box of necessities as a survival kit for that first day in the new home. It should include instant coffee, paper cups, eating utensils, a can opener, canned beverages, nonperishable snacks, a dishcloth, a hand towel, a coffee pot, a pan, and a first-aid kit. Have the movers pack it last so you have it first when the van arrives at the new address.

❦❦❦

More moving tips: Always place clean sheets and pillowcases in the dresser drawers. Then you can quickly make the beds as they are set up. The last thing to go in the moving van is the kitchen stool. Then when the van arrives at your new home, you can sit on the stool at the front door and direct the movers as to where to put the furniture. As the china and crystal are unpacked, immediately put them into their respective cabinets. They can always be removed and washed later. Carry an extra pair of shoes so you can change shoes several times during that hectic day.

This not only relieves your feet, but also helps to keep your disposition on an even keel amidst the turmoil.

❦

When you move or redecorate, place all screws, hooks, bolts, and so forth in separate plastic bags and tape each bag to the picture, bed, shelf, or utensil from whence it came. This will save a lot of time and frustration when you reassemble.

❦

Loose knobs on dresser drawers? Just detach and dip the screw portion in colorless nail polish or shellac before resetting them. When the shellac hardens, those screws will really be set, and I do mean really!

❦

If you are using shelf paper and thumb tacks for cabinets, buy a rubber crutch tip. Slip it over the head of your hammer so that you can pound the thumbtacks without chipping them.

CHAPTER 10

COLOR IT TRANQUIL

Painting is the intermediate somewhat between
a thought and a thing.
—Samuel Taylor Coleridge

Do-It-Yourself is the name of the game when it
comes to painting and decorating your home. One
small word of warning, however. Give a lot of thought
to the color of the paint or the choice of wallpaper.
You're going to live with it for a long time. Splash a bit
of paint on the walls. Let it dry. Live with it for a
couple of days. Still like it? Or, get an ample sample
of wallpaper. Attach it to the wall with tape. Let it
hang until you're sure you are very fond of it, or can't
stand it. Go wild, if you will, with reds and oranges,
except in the bedroom. Here you need the quiet colors
—clear greens, lovely blues, or neutral beiges. Could
have a lot to do with how well you sleep. I kid you
not!

If you invert a can of paint for a few days before you use it, you'll find it much easier to mix. A good, disposable paint mixer can be made from a wire coat hanger. Grab the middle of the horizontal bar of the hanger and pull until it is elongated. Then double the wire back toward the hook. You will have a mixer of four wire thicknesses with the book as a handle.

Place your paint can on a TV-tray stand with casters and avoid a lot of stooping. As you move, simply push the tray. You might poke several holes in the rim of the paint can using an ice pick and a hammer. The excess paint drips back into the can instead of accumulating around the rim. This is a fine idea if you plan to use the whole can, but if you always store your paint cans upside-down to prevent film, here is another method of preventing accumulation in that ridge. When opening a new can of paint, clean the top of the can and the cover of all excess paint. Then cut a piece of aluminum foil two inches wide and long enough to go around the top of the can, and fold into the can just a bit. This hides the ridge, and as you wipe your brush against the can to remove excess paint, it flows right into the can. When you've finished painting for the day, just peel off the foil, discard it, and replace the cover tightly.

Solve the problem of spray-painting screw heads by inserting them in an egg carton, or any box for that matter.

❦

Paint the finials of large wooden curtain rods by inserting the screw of the finial through an inverted berry basket, which is sturdy yet airy.

❦

Old-world charm is great in most rooms in a home, but pretty undesirable in the loo. A clawfoot bathtub may be a fine conversation piece, but it's just a pain in the elbow when it comes to keeping it clean. If the budget doesn't allow for new fixtures, ask your paint store about epoxy enamel. It's a remarkable paint that provides a hard finish and dries to the shiny look of porcelain.

❦

When painting baseboards, insert the lip of a clean dustpan as close to the bottom of the baseboard as possible. This protects carpets or floors from paint drips.

❦

Before painting the woodwork around windows, apply old-fashioned cake window cleaner to the glass. It gives you privacy while the shades are out being cleaned, and makes the removal of splattered paint very easy, and eliminates the tiresome job of scraping paint off the windows.

❦

Before putting the lid on a paint can, use a cotton swab to remove excess paint from the rim so the top won't stick.

❦

Before storing that partially used can of paint, slap a smidgen of the paint on the outside of the can so you can detect the color in a jiffy.

❦

Save the remains of paint cans in baby-food jars. They're so handy for touch-up jobs. You'd be surprised how many small places you can miss as you're painting and how many nicks you will find after the furniture is moved back into place.

❦

An old nylon is the perfect strainer for paint that has been standing for a long time. Cut a large hole in the center of a plastic coffee-can cover. Place a section of the nylon stocking over the empty coffee can and secure it with the cut-out cover. Pour the paint through the nylon into the can.

Here's an easy way to prevent the scum accumulation that appears on the top surface of partly used paints and varnishes. The plastic cover from a three-pound coffee can can be eased gently onto the lowered surface of the contents (of a gallon can). This floating cover prevents the captured air between the regular cover and the surface of the paint from forming the coating.

How do you clean that paintbrush? If you used a latex paint, wash the brush in warm suds and rinse thoroughly. For other types of paint, use a commercial solvent made for that purpose. Be sure to get all the paint out of the bristles. Then wash in warm suds, rinse, and hang the brush to dry. Whether it's a paintbrush used to paint pictures or the side of a barn, a little loving care will preserve the brush. Tie a string around the handle to hang it. When it's dry, wrap it in foil or put it in a plastic bag for storage.

Hot vinegar will clean paintbrushes quite well in case you run out of commercial cleaner or turpentine.

Tame paintbrush bristles by slipping a rubber band loosely over them while they dry after washing.

After washing paintbrushes, use a fabric softener for the final rinse. This leaves the brushes soft and pliable.

Here's a great way to dry paint rollers after you've washed them. Remove the cardboard section from a dry cleaner's wire coat hanger or snip the lower bar from a regular wire coat hanger. Bend the two long wires of the hanger down from the hook so they are parallel and can be inserted through the center of the roller. Now turn up the bottoms of the two wires just enough to secure the roller. Hang the hanger by its hook on a line or nail.

Never subject paintbrushes to detergent, whether they're the kind that are used to paint the bedroom walls or an immortal canvas. Cleanse them first in turpentine, then in warm soapy water (bar soap is effective as you can work the bristles into the bar). Rinse them thoroughly and allow to dry away from heat. A good paintbrush is a wise investment and will give you years of wear if treated kindly.

❦

Slip an old pair of knee-length socks over your hands to protect them from dripping paint. The socks will reach past your elbows.

❦

Bottled lemon juice removes paint odor from hands.

❦

Attach a paper towel holder with a roll of paper toweling to the underside of the top of your work ladder. You can't imagine how many paint drips this will prevent from spoiling an otherwise flawless job, not to mention how handy it is for cleaning windows, high cabinets, and woodwork.

❦

If you slip a pair of old socks over your shoes, they not only protect the shoes but, when you splatter a bit of paint on the floor, you can wipe it up easily with the sock-covered foot.

❦

Attach several large cup hooks to the top of your ladder for extra cloths within easy reach. Dip one cloth in turpentine, enclose it in a plastic bag, and hang it on one of the cup hooks. It will be handy for spills.

❦

If you've begun to feel like Henny Penny (she thought the sky was falling on her head) because the plaster on the ceiling is cracking, try this little trick. Mix some Elmer's glue with baking soda to form a paste. Apply it to the cracks with your finger. If the ceiling is colored, add a bit of food coloring to match. My skipper just patched up a bedroom ceiling, and I think we can postpone replastering for months.

❦

If you splatter paint on your favorite shift, or the skipper's shirt, remove as much paint as you can with a knife, then wash immediately. If the material is not washable, rub petroleum jelly into the paint spots and then soak in cleaning fluid. For paint spots that have set on washable fabrics, follow this jelly-cleaning fluid route, then wash.

❦

Working with wallpaper or rolls of adhesive-backed paper? Use an inverted stool to hold the rolls. Secure the rolls on the legs so they won't roll off a counter and unwind.

❦

Removing wallpaper is always a big job, no matter how you do it, but here's one way to "lighten the load," so to speak. Use a paint roller to soak the walls with hot water. It's much more effective than using a brush. After only two applications the paper peels off in sheets.

❦

When working with wallpaper cleaner, you'll find that it becomes moist from your hands. Knead in a bit of ordinary flour to bring the cleaner back to its proper consistency. By the way, wallpaper cleaner is a good substitute for modeling clay for the children to play with on a rainy day.

❦

A scratch on mahogany furniture can often be hidden by painting it with iodine.

❦

Ordinary brown shoe stain can be used to touch up furniture nicks if the colors are close to matching.

If a professional is doing the painting, have the closets painted first. Then, while the rooms are being painted, make use of the time by arranging the shelving in the closets.

Painting steps? Paint every other step, so that you can use the remaining ones. Paint the remainder when the first group are dry enough to use.

CHAPTER 11

TYKE TWISTS

Between the dark and the daylight
When the night is beginning to lower
Comes a pause in the day's occupation
That is known as the children's hour.
—Henry Wadsworth Longfellow,
"The Children's Hour"

Here's to all those wonderful mothers for whom the children's hour is more than sixty minutes. These tips should ease their burden, and some may start the little ones on a more independent existence.

A decorative way to keep a baby from slipping down in the high chair is to use those nonskid daisy flower designs that are made to be used in the bottom of bathtubs. Apply them to the seat of the high chair.

Cut a piece of the new carpeting used for the kitchen to fit your children's playpen. It works beautifully. You can wash up any spills, and crumbs and lint come up with the vacuum cleaner.

❦

Why is it the door bell rings most often when the baby is napping? Here is a subtle aid. Cut out a magazine picture of a sleeping baby. Mount it on cardboard and attach a little string that will allow it to hang right over the bell. With a felt pen, mark on the picture: "Baby sleeping. Please knock."

❦

If your baby "bubbles" a bit after his feedings, and it means many changes of garments during the day to keep him smelling sweet, try this: Moisten a cloth with water, dip it in baking soda, and dab at the dribble. Like magic, the odor will be removed. Don't go out (if you're taking the baby) without a damp "baking soda cloth" in a plastic bag.

❦

After washing your baby's bottle caps, nipples, and seals, place them in a clean berry basket to drain and dry. They would slip right through a big dish drainer, and these little baskets are the perfect size to hold them.

❦

Keep a toothbrush handy just to remove crumbs from kitchen chairs and the baby's high chair. The toothbrush will get down into the crevices.

❧❧

No baby scale? Weigh yourself on your bathroom scale while you are holding the baby. Then put baby down, weigh yourself. Subtract!

❧❧

If your baby won't cooperate when you want to put his arms in the sleeves of his snowsuit, the whole procedure is much easier for both of you if you first turn the sleeve inside out, reach through the sleeve with your own hand, grasp his little hand, and then turn the sleeve right side out onto his arm. Since you are holding his hand, he no longer has the chance to grab the material and hang on for "dear life".

❧❧

A tip for harried mothers: Spray furniture-polish works wonders on shoes for those times when you're five minutes late for church and Junior comes in with scuffed shoes. Spray and wipe for a ten-second shine.

❧❧

Use a black felt-tipped pen to cover the scuff marks on your children's shoes. Put a coat of black polish on the shoes and buff them. They'll look almost as good as new. These felt pens come in so many colors that any color shoe can be "renewed" by this method.

Some of the space of the space of

If your children wear thonged sandals during the summer, in order to help them to know which is for the left foot and which for the right, draw a little face on the sandals—half the face on one sandal and half on the other. When the face fits together properly, the sandals are in the right position to be put on.

Some of the space of

Attach a two-inch strip of bright colored tape across the back seams of children's boots to identify them easily at school, meetings, etc. and to prevent boot mix-up and loss. Teach the children to button the top button of any coat that is hung on a public coat rack. It prevents the coat from slipping off and also deters anyone from grabbing the wrong coat, as so often happens.

Some of the space of

Another boot hint for stormy days. Using a marker pen, mark an X on the inside of the children's boots.

Even the smallest tyke can learn that if the X is on the inside when he dons a boot, it will be on the right foot.

❦

Sew a loop of elastic thread inside each cuff of your boy's or girl's sweaters. Slip this loop over the child's thumb when you put on his coat. The sweater sleeves then stay in place instead of riding up.

❦

A simple idea that will save you many a precious moment on busy winter mornings: Purchase a shoe-bag and hang it on the back of the closet door that is near your entrance. Teach the children to put their mittens together into the pockets of the shoebag. Even the skipper can put his chore gloves and ear muffs into a pocket. Sure saves a lot of frantic searching.

❦

When you take the children to a movie or any public gathering, bring along a large shopping bag. Before going to your seats, collect all the mittens, scarves, hats, etc., and place them in the shopping bag. It saves a lot of trouble searching for lost items when it's time to go home.

❦

Put your child's initials on a snap clothespin with nail polish. He can use it at school to snap his boots together.

❧⚜❧

A hint mainly to mothers of small children who enjoy rolling in the snow: After putting the children into their snow pants, slip a plastic bag over each shoe and partway up the leg. Secure them with rubber bands large enough so as not to stop circulation. Fold down the excess plastic and put on the boots. The snow usually gets into the boots, but shoes and socks will never get wet.

❧⚜❧

Children are more apt to learn orderliness if their dresser drawers are marked so they can easily identify the contents. Cut out brightly colored pictures of shirts, blouses, socks, etc., from magazines. Paste the pictures to the dresser drawers. If you lacquer over the drawings, they become attractive designs, and the children learn easily where each item of clothing is kept.

❧⚜❧

A tip to prevent the little kittens from losing their mittens: Sew snaps on the inner cuffs of the mittens and teach the tykes to snap the mittens together as soon as they remove them.

⚜

A long pole suspended with two elongated wire coat hangers from the conventional pole will provide an easy-to-reach bar for the little ones who are trained to hang up their own clothes.

⚜

A child's plastic wading pool is just the right size to invert to cover the sandbox when it is not in use. It protects the sand and keeps it a much more sanitary area for the children's play. Anchor the pool with a brick so it won't blow over.

⚜

Use metal shower-curtain rings as locks for the yard gate. Little fingers can't open them, yet it's quick and easy for you to unsnap them.

⚜

An efficient young mother told me her greatest aids on a motoring trip are a roll of paper towels and a roll of plastic bags. The bags can be used to tuck away small toys and crayons after the tykes have tired of them. They can hold candy bars and cookies after little appetites are satisfied. The paper towels wipe faces and hands, take care of spills, and clean the windshield as well.

❦

If your little girl's hair has finally grown to the ponytail length, but taking out the rubber band that secures it causes tears when it pulls her hair, use those leftover tie-bands that come with the plastic bags, instead.

❦

The old problem of gathering up all the toys when day is done is still with us. A large plastic garbage pail can be used as a toy container. The kids will learn to deposit their playthings in it. It can be kept outdoors, too, since it has a cover.

❦

A new brightly colored plastic dustpan should be inside every child's toy box. When cleanup time arrives, the tyke will actually enjoy scooping up small toys, crayons, and parts of games and puzzles with the dustpan and returning them to the toy box.

❦

Sew a plastic curtain ring to each small toy and try to teach the children to hang the toys on easy-to-reach hooks in their room.

A purchase of potatoes can save a mother of small children a lot of headaches—not by eating the potatoes, but by making use of the bags that they come in. Ten pounds of potatoes come in nice strong net sacks. After they are washed, these sacks become toy sacks for playthings. Your child can easily see through the sacks to find what she wants. It keeps the toy box neat. The bags can be hung on hooks if no toy box is used.

Plastic dishpans can hold Junior's toys, too. You might have the skipper of your household ship build some shelves, and the littlest member of your crew will delight (I hope) in picking up his toys and storing them in the dishpans that fit onto the shelves. When the family takes off for a motoring trip, simply cart along one of the dishpans to keep the little hands and minds busy.

Pipe cleaners are ideal toys for little tykes. They can shape them into animals, dolls, etc.

To make sturdy playing blocks for children, rinse and dry empty milk cartons, cut off the hood tops, and insert one into the other, so that they form solid blocks. Use all sizes. They are light enough for little hands to manage and the blocks hold up quite well. And the price is right!

Before joining the two carton sections, you might insert several empty spools, jingle bells, or an old rattle. Cover the joined cartons with gay fabric, featuring animals, flowers, bright stripes, or polka dots. Use yarn to whip-stitch the seams together. They also make "fun gifts" for very little time—and even less money.

Pretty colored plastic snap clothespins save a lot of bending to retrieve bathroom towels that have fallen to the floor. When you hang a towel on one rod, allow about three inches of it to hang over the rod in the back and the rest to hang neatly in the front. Snap the pins on either side of each towel to secure it. Children can dash into the bathroom, wash and dry hands in a hurry, and the towel does not slip to the floor.

Use a plastic margarine tub in the bathtub as a floating soap dish for your child. It will help him remember to put the soap back into the "boat," which makes it easier to find and also saves the soap a bit.

Help your child distinguish between hot and cold water faucets at the sink by marking the hot-water tap with red adhesive tape and the cold-water tap with blue tape.

❦❦❦

Cottage-cheese cartons make excellent party hats. Paste different shades of colored crepe paper on the cartons. Punch holes at either side and use string or ribbon for ties.

❦❦❦

If you don't want to make holes in the walls or wood-work with thumb tacks or mark the walls with tape when the children play "pin the tail on the donkey," get a very large cardboard box and stand it on end. Tape the donkey to the box. It will also be simpler for the children to push the pins (which hold the tails) through it. This makes for a movable game so it can be played anywhere in the house.

❦❦❦

An effective and very inexpensive way to keep toddlers out of kitchen cabinets is to use shower curtain hooks (the type that snap shut). Two hooks interlocked to handles of a cabinet will prevent little hands from grabbing dangerous cleaning agents.

❦❦❦

Give the children some plastic bags to take to school to cover their books in case of rain.

❦❦❦

Use your egg timer when taking Junior's temperature. Not only does it tell you when the three minutes are up, but the running sands will fascinate your tyke while he has to sit still.

❦❦❦

Here is a tip for young mothers who live in houses. Place a clock face out in the window, so that the youngsters can check on the time. They won't have to run into the house asking if it's time for lunch or time to come in, and it will save wiping up foot tracks.

❦❦❦

If your organization or church group is planning a big family picnic, here's a name-tag tip: Place the children's name tags on their backs. Then there is no temptation for them to tear the tags off!

❦❦❦

Your adjustable ironing board will provide a fine extra table for the little tykes when you have guests. Place it low enough for their convenience and cover it with plastic or cotton cloth.

Having the right change for the children when they need it for milk at school or day camp, or for ice cream or the movies, is a constant problem. Keep an empty coffee can in a cupboard in the kitchen. When you come home from shopping, deposit all the change that you have in your purse in the can. When your husband returns each evening, have him do the same. Not only is it a big help for the children's needs, but you can also use the change can for bus fares and miscellaneous expenditures.

CHAPTER 12

A NUDGE FROM NATURE

There is a pleasure in the pathless woods,
There is a rapture on the lonely shore,
There is society, where none intrudes,
By the deep sea, and music in its roar,
I love not man the less, but Nature more.
　　　　　　　　　　—Lord Byron

Every housedoll should get a B.E. degree—like in bachelor of ecology. Now mind you, I don't mean for you to drop the mop and dash off to the nearest university. Just issue a few sharp directives to that crew of yours and set a good example.

If we're going to clean up this old planet of ours and make it livable again, there's no better place for the campaign to start than right in the home with the champion cleaner-upper of all time: the American wife and mother. Right? Ecology, according to my *American Heritage Dictionary of the English Language*, means "the science of the relationships between organisms and their environments." All of which boils down to putting the right thing in the right place and keeping the wrong thing where it belongs, and we're experts at that, aren't we?

❧⚜❧

Here are ten guidelines to help you and your family depollute Mother Earth:

1. Start an antilitter campaign in your neighborhood. If you see someone throw a piece of paper or anything else on the street, look him in the eye and say, "Didn't you just drop something?"

2. Phosphates from detergents are polluting our lakes and rivers. Use soap instead. Our grandmothers' wash loads looked great, and they used plain old yellow laundry soap. If you have an automatic washer, use only the amount of detergent marked on the package. Switch to a mild soap for excellent hair and skin care. You'll find it is much kinder to your mane and hide than detergents.

3. Buy products in cardboard or paper containers. They degrade easily. If you must buy plastic containers, keep the containers and make things from them. Polyvinyl chloride (soft plastic) gives off harmful fumes when incinerated.

4. Form a Smokers Anonymous group. If you and your friends all quit smoking at the same time, you'll not only stop polluting the air, but you'll also gain a big plus factor for life expectancy.

5. The minute you see black smoke pouring out of a smokestack, run to the nearest telephone and report it to the authorities.

6. Never, never use DDT to spray your garden or

lawn. And, of course, you wouldn't think of burning leaves or debris, now, would you?

7. Your auto is a big polluter. For short distances, leave the car in the garage, and bicycle or walk. You'll become a healthy, happy depolluter!

8. If you take a long trip by car take litter bags with you. Caution the little ones not to throw anything out of the car windows.

9. Become a noise-abatement bug by bugging your teen-ager to lower the stereo or radio sound level.

10. Conserve our natural resources. Don't let water run if you're not using it. Reuse aluminum TV trays and pie pans. Return wire coat hangers to your cleaner. Or better yet, make things from them. I did a TV show for years based on bending wire coat hangers into usable objects. Bend the wire and bend your mind to creating and conserving. Be aware! Think ecology!

❦

Empty sifter-type herb jars make splendid containers for garden seeds. You get only the amount you need as you shake the seeds into the earth furrows. They're also fine for dispensing grass seed in small areas.

❦

Make a weed-puller by driving two nails into the tip of a broom handle. Tape the tip of the handle before hammering so the wood will not split. The heads of the nails, when sunk into the ground and twisted, will pull the weeds out quickly.

❦

Hook a clothes pin bag to the handle of your lawn mower. Use it to hold the stones, twigs, and other garden debris that you pick up so that they won't get into the mower. Bend the wire hook of the bag over the mower handle and tie the bottom of the bag to the shaft of the mower.

❦

Your garden tools will remain rust-free if you store them in a bucket of sand to which you have added oil.

❦

Use a beer-can opener to remove those pesky weeds that pop up in the cracks of your sidewalk.

❦

Are you the type who likes to scare away bunnies? Now, c'mon, you know what I mean—those fresh little rabbits that come into your garden and eat the vegetables before you do. Make a bunny-scarer. Cut the bottom from a two-pound coffee tin. With tin shears, shape it into a pinwheel. Bend the blades so that they'll spin. Drive a nail through the center of the tin pinwheel to attach it to a stump or a block of wood. Allow the nail to protrude so the wheel will have enough play to revolve in the wind. No bunnies!

❦

Vacationing in a camper or generally roughing it during the summer? Here are some handy tips. A two-gallon thermos jug with a spigot is a source of hot running water. Keep a plastic basin under the spigot to catch any drippings. Save foil pie tins, margarine tubs, TV dinner trays, and styrofoam meat trays throughout the year. They become sturdy and washable dishes. A child's broom is just the right size to sweep out a camper. Use lap trays for the children to use for their coloring books while traveling.

❦

Does Junior's bike block your approach to the garage? This happened once too often in one family, so they used red paint to mark off spaces on the garage floor. The entire area was marked "parking space" and smaller areas were marked with the children's names. The youngsters were very good about using their "parking places" for sleds during the winter and had just as much fun parking their bikes. Your skipper will have no trouble driving his car into the garage without obstructions if you adopt this plan.

❦

There's a set of divining rods on the market that will help you locate on old well, a lost cistern, or water pipes on your property. Save your pennies. You can make your own dowsing delights with two wire coat hangers.

Snap the hooks from the hangers with a wire cutter. Then straighten the wires into L shapes. The smaller part of the L should be about eight inches long and the longer section about twenty-four inches. Hold the divining rods by the shorter sections, one in each hand, allowing the longer parts of the wires to extend in front of you. The wires should be in a horizontal position and parallel to each other. Now, walk very slowly over any ground where there may be enclosed water underground. Use a slow shuffling step. Do not grasp the rods so tightly that they will not turn in your hand, because that is exactly what they will do as you approach water. When you stand over the underground water, the rods will turn inward and meet. Honest Injun!

Two percent of the population has an insensitivity barrier. For them, this will not work. Five percent is partially insensitive. But for 93 percent of us, it works like a charm. Why not make up a whole batch of divining rods and have a dowsing party? Great way to liven up an outing.

❦

Attach a small shelf or a bracket just outside your back door so you'll have a place to put your packages while you fumble for the key.

❦

Keep in your car a few of the long plastic bags in which bread comes. When it rains, slip your umbrella into the bags. No more puddles in the car.

❦

An ideal parking place for those slush-soaked boots. Line a big box with rubber shelf cushioning that is sold by the yard. Place it at the back door and instruct all the members of the family to deposit wet boots, rubbers, and umbrellas in it before entering the house. It's so easy to clean. Just go over the rubber shelving with a damp cloth.

❦

Ever try to thaw out the lock on your automobile on a cold morning? Try this. When the temperature drops to freezing, place a piece of adhesive tape over the lock before leaving the car out for the night. It is easily removed, and you won't have to cope with a frozen lock.

❦

Don't run the risk of leaving the headlights on and running down the car battery. Here's a little trick. On gloomy days when you must put the lights on even though it's still daylight, put a little reminder on the pull-out gadget that controls the lights—a handkerchief or tissue or even a glove. (Better a cold hand than a run-down battery.) Then, when you park the car, you'll remember to turn off the lights.

⋙⋘

Freeze blocks of ice in empty milk containers and cottage cheese cartons, and take them along in the boat on fishing trips. As the day goes on, they melt a bit, and the ice in the cheese cartons comes out in a chunk and is placed in the minnow buckets. Chip the ice in the milk cartons to use with drinking water or soft drinks and still have enough ice to place around the fish to keep it fresh.

⋙⋘

Attach the lid of a baby-food jar to the bottom of a rural mailbox. Place the paper boy's money in the baby-food jar and secure it to the lid. Tell the paper boy to leave your receipts in the jar. Paint the jar and the lid the same color as the mailbox.

⋙⋘

Are you motoring a thousand miles with cousin Jane, who is a chain smoker? Is Junior an adventurous kid who roams into poison-ivy patches? Does your skipper always manage to start a grease fire when he barbecues? You can meet many a summer emergency with a package of baking soda! Put a scoop into the car's ashtrays so cousin Jane can safely snuff out her cigarettes. It will absorb the stale smoke odors, too. You can also use a bit of the soda on a wet cloth to clean the windshield, windows, and headlights. Apply a thick paste of baking soda and water to Junior's insect bites and poison-ivy rashes to relieve the itching. Before skipper absolutely ruins the steaks, put out the grease fire by throwing handfuls of baking soda onto the base of the fire. Deodorize your vacuum bottles, picnic coolers, jugs, and ice chests with a solution of warm water and baking soda. And if the long, hot summer has been just too much, grab a package of baking soda. Dump it into a tubful of tepid water. Choose a nice, romantic novel. Tell the family to fend for themselves for a while so you can loll in the tub, reading, until your drooping spirits are revived. Happy lolling.

CHAPTER 13

EXTRA GROOVY GIMMICKS

Our life is frittered away by detail. . . .
Simplify, simplify.
　　　　　—Henry David Thoreau, *Walden*

You heard what the man said. . . .

Many creams and cosmetics are placed on sale once or twice a year. Mark the purchase date right on the product's label when you buy it. This way you won't miss the sales. It tells you how long a particular bottle or jar lasts and indicates the quantity to buy at the next sale.

Here is a happy solution for those who live in small apartments and have a long trip downstairs to dispose of their garbage. Keep a plastic bowl with a very tight lid on the drainboard. Line it with the plastic produce bags received at the market. The bag is water-proof and there is no odor in the kitchen because of the tight lid. The bag travels downstairs neatly without leaking.

Tired of hunting for the end of the transparent tape? Try this trick. After using the tape, attach a plastic tab from a bread bag to the end of the tape. It's easy to find the end and there's no more sticking to the roll.

Keep that ball of twine handy in an empty coffee can. Cut a small hole in the center of the plastic lid and pull the end of the twine through. Snap the lid back in place. Place a large rubber band around the can and tuck in a small pair of scissors.

Is the grout between the tiles above your bathtub exuding mildew? The easiest way to beat the mildew blues is to paint the grout and the caulking around the sink with liquid porcelain repair. It comes in a bottle with a little brush that makes for quick application.

Those triangular plastic strainers designed to use in a corner of the kitchen sink are also useful in the bathroom. They fit neatly at the corner of the tub and hold the soap, sponge, pumice stone, and a small can of cleanser.

❦

When gluing broken china or glass, do you have difficulty inserting the broken piece in exactly the right position? Try this little trick: Place the broken piece into place before applying the glue. When it's fitted into place, draw several lines across the broken piece and the container, cup, vase, or whatever it may be. Use a water-soluble marking pen. Then after the glue is applied, you can match the pieces perfectly and remove the lines when the glue hardens. No more goofs!

❦

Keep those medicine bottles from tipping over on a bedside table. Cut holes in the bottom of a small cardboard box. Invert the box and insert the bottles.

❦

Are you a magazine-page tearer? The next time you spot a page with a good recipe, a snazzy fashion picture, or a delectable color scheme, use the paper-clip-and-thread trick. Tie a long length of thread to the paper clip. Secure the clip to the top of the page you wish to tear. Now run the thread along the inside of the page, as close to the binding as possible. Turn the page and gently pull up on the string. The page will neatly part from the magazine.

❦

If a lamp cord is too long and trailing all over the floor, you can do a very neat shortening job by wrapping the excess cord around a broom handle. Slip a pipe cleaner or a tie-band through the spiraled cord and twist it. Don't twist it too tightly or you might injure the coating on the cord and have a fire hazard. Don't forget to remove the broom handle!

So many beautiful place mats made of plastic, vinyl, or straw are on the market today, but they do present a storage problem. Some do not fit well in the kitchen drawers, and stuffing them in makes them curl. Hang them with trouser hangers, clipping each set together on one hanger. They can be kept on the inside of cabinet doors.

If two drinking glasses stick together, one inside the other, fill the top glass with cold water and set the bottom glass in hot water and they'll come apart.

Inexpensive plastic buckets are a boon. Keep one filled with soap powder in the laundry room. No more wet-bottomed boxes. In winter another bucket can be kept near the doorway to hold rock salt. Use a plastic cup for easy dipping. Icy sidewalks are made salt-safe in a jiffy.

A ski instructor at Sun Valley, Idaho, used this method to retrieve a contact lens from the snow. With his ski pole, he drew a circle around the area where the student had dropped the lens. He sent for a pail and shovel. Shovels of snow were allowed to melt in the pail. Besides the lens, he found a pearl button, a bus token, and a false eyelash!

People who engage in active sports and wear glasses have a problem in common. The glasses often slip down their noses, and they spend a good deal of time pushing the glasses back into place. A simple solution: Purchase a length of rubber surgical tubing (available at any store where surgical supplies are sold). Cut two pieces, about one-half inch in length, and slip them on the ends of each temple piece. The material is slightly tacky but soft enough not to irritate the back of the ear. Even when playing tennis in very hot weather, there is no slippage.

If you carry ball-point pens in your purse, you know you are always digging around to find them. What's worse, they often mark the purse's lining. Use an old eyeglass case and clip the pens to the inside of the case. They are easy to find, and no more danger of ugly pen marks.

You know how difficult it is to find your keys in your purse, especially when your arms are loaded with bundles. Make a pompom of yarn and attach it to your key chain. It doesn't take up much space in your purse and enables you to find the keys in a jiffy.

For those of you who have only two or three keys on a chain, don't forget to mark the front-door key with a dab of red nail polish. This saves a lot of guesswork when you're trying to open the door in a hurry. Mark the auto ignition key in the same way so you can distinguish it from the trunk key.

If you don't have a small funnel on hand to use when filling small-mouthed salt and pepper shakers, tear off the corner of an envelope. Snip a bit of paper from the tip of the corner, and you have a fine substitute.

For anyone who doesn't have or doesn't want an umbrella stand, here's a good way to store umbrellas. Simply hang a towel bar behind a door or in a closet. You can hang a lot of umbrellas on it. If an umbrella doesn't have a curved handle, a shower-curtain hook suspended from the bar can be attached to the leather thong that is meant for toting the umbrella by the wrist.

Attractive wicker baskets are so fashionable these days. I cherish them for holding flowers, and two empty baskets will save a lot of trips up and down the stairs. Keep one at the top of the stairs and another at the foot of the staircase. They hold so many little things that have to be transported up or down and which can be carried in one fell swoop in the baskets.

❦

You won't miss a telephone call while you are working down in the basement if you remember to set your telephone in a dishpan before you go downstairs. Place it on the floor. The ring will be amplified so that you can hear it loud and clear!

❦

If the telephone book takes up too much room, straddle it on the bar of a wire coat hanger and hang it on a hook. Tape two hangers together for strength if need be.

❦

Remember the trick of rubbing the point of a lead pencil on the teeth of a stubborn zipper? Well, this treatment works for electric plugs that won't pull out of the socket easily. Rub the prongs with the lead of a pencil. It's the graphite content that acts as a lubricant.

❦

Address and stamp several envelopes to yourself to give to your college-bound offspring. This insures hearing from her often. Place your address stickers on the back for insurance.

❦

The next time you send coins in the mail, use a matchbook from which the matches have been removed. Tape the coins inside. They'll be protected and won't slide through the envelope.

❦

When you get postage stamps out of a machine, save the folded cardboard protectors to use when you put coins in the mail. Secure the coins with tape before placing them in the envelope.

❦

Save the flaps from old envelopes that have not been sealed. They make fine labels for storage boxes, jars, etc.

❦

When you finish using a box of stationery, you probably have envelopes left over. Here's a use for those leftover envelopes. Open the glued ends very carefully so they don't tear. Write your informal notes to close friends on the inside of the envelope; refold the envelope, moisten the flap, address, and mail.

We could all get a lot more out of our shopping dollars if we took the time to read the labels on the products that we buy. For instance, on that simple little box of baking soda, you will find that it cleans and sweetens your refrigerator, keeps plastic dinnerware looking like new, cleans combs and brushes, soothes minor burns and scalds, and relieves acid indigestion. Besides all those little wonders it does for your baking.

A struck match is one of the best deodorants for a room. Allow the match to burn for a few seconds and then blow it out and wave the burnt match in the air. Great to rid your kitchen of the smell of cooked fish or cabbage!

A few drops of cologne in the water of your humidifier will impart a delightful scent throughout the room. Groovy idea if that certain fellow is coming to call! To instill fragrance in any small area, such as lingerie drawers or linen cabinets, punch several holes in the top of a plastic pill bottle. Then stuff a small wad of cotton in the bottom of the bottle. Pour a bit of your cologne into the cotton. Recap, and the scent will exude through the holes.

❦

Put leftover soap slivers into the clothes hamper so that it always smells fresh and clean. If you place them in your linen cabinet they impart a just-washed fragrance to the sheets and towels.

❦

Linens such as fancy guest towels that are not used often gather soil in the linen closet. Keep them in a plastic box and they are always fresh and clean when you need them.

❦

When pouring liquid from a can that has an off-center opening, such as a turpentine can, hold the can so that the opening is topside. It's much easier to control the flow.

❦

If you have the problem of sleeping with a husband who pulls the blankets off you during the night, try this—buy a baby-blanket fastener. Tie it to the frame of the bed on your side. When you retire, clip it to the edge of the blanket. No matter how often he turns and pulls on the blanket during the night, it stays secure. These same baby blanket fasteners (used in pairs) are the solution for retaining those slippery down or Dacron comforters.

Another way to keep a satin comforter from slipping off the bed at night. Sew an elastic band about two inches wide at the foot of the comforter on the underside. Instead of tucking the comforter in, slip the elastic under the mattress. No more chilled awakenings in the middle of the night.

Here is a home-nursing hint that can be used when the doctor orders hot applications. Place the cloth in a potato ricer and then dip it in scalding water, ricer and all. The water can be squeezed out quickly with the ricer, and your hands are protected from the heat.

Candle stubs are fine to use to start fires in the fireplace. They're also the handiest waxers in the world when a drawer sticks. Just rub one along the sides of the drawer.

Sorting checks for income-tax purposes will be a lot easier next year if you adopt this method when you start your new checkbooks. Whenever you write a check that is for a deductible payment, underline your signature with red pencil. Also mark your check stub with the red pencil. You'll be able to flip through a pile of canceled checks and your checkbook in very little time to find your deductible items.

❦

Before starting to bake, wrap a piece of clear plastic wrap around the telephone receiver. Doesn't it always ring when your hands are sticky with dough? Put some around the door knob, just in case you have to open the door for someone. At clean up time, just peel off the wrap and discard.

❦

Have you spent a lot of time and energy removing the sticky residue after tearing away the price tag on pots, pans, plastic containers, and leather goods? A little peanut butter rubbed into the spot allows you to wipe it clean in an instant. The peanut-butter trick works equally well on kids if you have to remove tar, the residue from an adhesive bandage, or gum out of hair.

❦

Make a diagram of your fuse box on a piece of sturdy cardboard. Mark which fuse is which—"dining room," "front bedroom," etc. Paste this on a wall close to your fuse box. Keep a flashlight handy just in case the fuse-box room's fuse blows!

⚜

Now and then we still run across a can of goodies with the key attached to the bottom. Often we lose that little key. Tape six bobby pins together, side by side. It will substitute for the lost key.

⚜

Photos that curl can be straightened by running them through a typewriter roll against the curl.

⚜

Scrapbook or photo-album pages sticking? Place a sheet of waxed paper between the pages right after you paste an item in the book.

⚜

Old photograph albums with plastic enclosures for snapshots sometimes tend to stick together, especially if they have been kept in too warm a place. Sprinkle cornstarch between the pages and move them to a cooler spot. No more sticking!

⚜

If the batteries on the flashbulb camera weaken, just moisten the ends of the flashbulb slightly before attaching. You'll probably get three or four more flashes before the batteries give out. Sometimes the contact is faulty because the ducts that hold the batteries are clogged. These can be cleaned in an instant with the eraser end of a pencil.

❦

Hi, skippers! Frustrated by your last golf score? Take it out on your clubs by giving them a good cleaning. Use paste wax on the woods and fine-grade steel wool on the pitted areas of the irons and on the shafts of all the clubs. Can't tell—this might even put new sparkle in your game!

❦

Rubber gloves will last longer if you reinforce the fingertips so your nails won't poke through. Invert the gloves and place patches of adhesive tape on the vulnerable tips.

INDEX